The Handbook for Developing Supportive Learning Environments

Teddy Holtz Frank

Routledge
Taylor & Francis Group
LONDON AND NEW YORK

First published 2005 by Eye on Education

Published 2013 by Routledge
2 Park Square, Milton Park, Abingdon, Oxon OX14 4RN
711 Third Avenue, New York, NY, 10017, USA

Routledge is an imprint of the Taylor & Francis Group, an informa business

Library of Congress Cataloging-in-Publication Data

Frank, Teddy Holtz.

The handbook for developing supportive learning environments / TeddyHoltz Frank.

p. cm.

Includes bibliographical references.

ISBN 1-59667-013-4

1. School improvement programs— Handbooks, manuals, etc. 2.School environment—Handbooks, manuals, etc. I. Title.

LB2822.8.F73 2005

371.2—dc22

2005017150

ISBN 13: 978-1-596-67013-6 (pbk)

Editorial and production services provided by Richard H. Adin Freelance Editorial Services

Also Available from EYE ON EDUCATION

Helping Students Graduate:
A Strategic Approach to Dropout Prevention
Jay Smink and Franklin P. Schargel

Dropout Prevention Tools
Franklin P. Schargel

Strategies to Help Solve Our School Dropout Problem
Franklin P. Schargel and Jay Smink

At-Risk Students
Reaching and Teaching Them, Second Edition
Richard Sagor and Jonas Cox

Student Transitions from Middle to High School:
Improving Achievement and Creating a Safer Environment
J. Allen Queen

Applying Standards-Based Constructivism
A Two Step Guide for
Motivating Middle and High School Students
Flynn, Mesibov, Vermette, and Smith

Applying Standards-Based Constructivism
A Two Step Guide for Motivating Elementary School Students
Flynn, Mesibov, Vermette, and Smith

Dealing with Difficult Parents
(And with Parents in Difficult Situations)
Whitaker and Fiore

101 "Answers" for New Teachers and Their Mentors:
Effective Teaching Tips for Daily Classroom Use
Breaux

Self-Efficacy: Raising the Bar for All Students, Second Edition
Joanne Eisenberger, Marcia Conti-D'Antonio,
and Robert Bertrando

20 Strategies for Collaborative School Leaders
Jane Clark Lindle

Foreword

Anyone who has worked with Teddy Holtz Frank recognizes that she is articulate, intelligent, perceptive, and passionate about helping children and schools improve. *The Handbook for Developing Supportive Learning Environments* demonstrates these attributes.

Teddy offers the reader a comprehensive assessment of what is currently taking place in education as well as a model for improvement. As she writes, "We must have the moral courage to look deeper than the symptoms of low academic achievement, high school dropouts and teen pregnancy to examine the real root causes." And believe me, Teddy has the moral courage.

Educators have seen a dramatic increase in the number of at-risk learners, students placed in special education, and school dropouts and yet few have developed a process to reduce these factors. This book describes a process.

The book is more than a "what to do" document. It shows you "how to do it". Teachers, counselors and administrators appreciate the "what to do," but need the "how to do it." With its action plans, flowcharts, eco-maps and web resources, this book develops a clear roadmap that is easy for all to follow.

Teddy Holtz Frank has not glossed over the fact that it is difficult to establish a supportive learning environment. Her book is a call to action to those who wish to improve the state of education. I urge all who read it to go forth and do likewise.

Franklin P. Schargel
Albuquerque, NM

Acknowledgements

I would like to acknowledge the many people who have been instrumental in the course of my career in offering their support and friendship and in helping me shape my thoughts and ideas. First and foremost, I would like to thank Franklin Schargel for being such a wonderful mentor and friend to me. Thanks to my publisher, Bob Sickles for his contributions to quality education and for taking the time to listen and learn. Thanks to Assistant Commissioner, Jim Butterworth for his pragmatic and visionary leadership in closing the achievement gap, to Becky Gardner for her insistence and persistence about supportive learning environments, and to Mary Jalloh for her unflappable navigation in a sea of constant crisis and change. Thanks to Jane Bullowa for her listening ear and guidance, to Lucy Barbera for her friendship and wisdom, to my colleagues on the Diversity Work Group for stepping up, and special thanks to Michelle Bridgewater for her sisterhood, calm strength, and quiet vision which makes it all seem possible.

To my fellow coordinators on the Student Support Team, to my colleagues at the New York State Center for School Safety, to my staff at the Hudson Valley Student Support Services, to Clarence Cooper and Marge Bell, thanks for keeping the faith in our young people and families.

To Kathy Quaranta, Vinnie Giordano, Carmine DeBetta, Vicki Dennis, Barbara Dominick and my original training team at SPARK, to my colleagues at the BEST Foundation and Project ALERT, to Kathy Coughlin and Roberta Blotner, my thanks to all of you for believing in the power of prevention.

Thanks also to my dear friend, Sandy Bernabei, for her unflagging devotion to social justice, to my colleagues in the Anti-Racist Alliance, and to the People's Institute for Survival and Beyond, especially Ron Chisom, Reverend David Billings and Margery Freeman for their lifetime of work in undoing racism.

And finally, to my husband Dennis, whose love and support is my rock, to my sons David and Justin, the lights in my eye, to my sisters Beth and Karin for their resilience and ageless wisdom, and to my Mom, who was my original teacher and who teaches me still.

This book is dedicated in loving memory to Jonathan, and to those who have come before us and paved the way so that all of our children might lead fuller, more peaceful lives in this place we call home.

Table of Contents

Introduction

We must look into the underlying structures which shape individual actions and create the conditions where types of events become more likely.

Peter Senge

The Achievement Gap: An Uncensored Look

Schools are not isolated institutions. They reflect the norms of the dominant culture and society, the culture of power (Delpit, 1995; Kohl, 1994; Miller, 1976; Payne, 1996; Tatum, 1991). These norms and hidden rules have historically created disparate results for different groups of people (Chisom & Washington, 1997; Noguera, 2003). In education, we euphemistically refer to this disparity as the achievement gap.

If it was once said that some students fall through the cracks, it must now be acknowledged that the crack has become a chasm separating those who will succeed from those who will not. The academic achievement gap has become wide enough to engulf whole communities and populations of students. These so-called subpopulations of students are not random; they follow a sad and predictable pattern of social inequities. They are most often poor children and children of color. Neither they nor their families have received their fair chance to engage in high-quality education, the stepping-stone to the American Dream. These are the children who have been left behind.

If we are to address this gap, we must address these racial and economic disparities in achievement. We must start by having an honest conversation about racism and poverty, and about how these constructs have created the institutional barriers to access that continue to plague our lowest-performing schools and students. We cannot fix these disparities by trying to fix the learners. We have tried that and we have failed.

We must have the moral courage to look deeper than the symptoms of low academic achievement, high school dropouts, and teen pregnancy to examine the real root causes. We must analyze the system of power within the institution of education and actively remove the savage inequalities underlying the achievement gap (Kozol, 1991). We must move beyond ignorance, denial, and defensiveness and work together to create supportive learning communities that provide a fighting chance for our students. It is time to create a more equitable educational system in America—one in which all children are valued and given opportunities to develop their full human potential.

A Definition of Supportive Learning Environments

Learning is essentially a social activity. Schools are, after all, social environments. Yet, we often think of learning as a solitary activity, something that happens in the learner's head. When we focus on education, we tend to view students in isolation and ignore the context in which learning takes place. The actual process of learning is influenced most strongly by the environment created for learning.

Think for a moment about the daily realities of the school environment. Elements of the environment include the quality of relationships between teachers and students, and students and students; the school climate; the sense of belonging, bonding and connection that students feel to their school and learning; the safety of the physical environment; the communication between school and home; the involvement of the parents in their child's learning; the role of community in providing connections between real life and learning; the opportunities in the classroom for active participation; and self-direction and autonomy in the learning process itself. All these elements directly relate to the context in which learning takes place and significantly affect the learners' experience.

This context is what we mean by supportive learning environments. It can be defined as "The intentional creation of a challenging, supportive, and relevant learning community that allows all learners to achieve at their highest potential." Our goal for developing supportive learning environments is to increase student achievement and success in all domains: intellectual, emotional, social, spiritual, and academic. As you will see in our review of the elements of supportive learning environments (see Chapter 3), this context encompasses all aspects of the learning experience.

Why Focus on Supportive Learning Environments?

There are many common misconceptions about supportive learning environments. Business sometimes erroneously refers to hard skills—such as accounting, marketing, and sales—versus soft skills—such as human resource issues, management, and relationship skills. In education we have created a similar dichotomy between academic components and nonacademic components of learning. I have worked in many schools that create separate teams to deal with curriculum and instruction and associated staff development. These are certainly key areas in teaching and learning. The problem occurs when the so-called nonacademic issues largely get ignored or relegated to the lowest-level priority. These contextual elements pertain to staff and student relationships, classroom management, discipline, safety, multicultural competence, and parent and community involvement. Many schools misperceive that these issues are somehow separate from student achievement in mathematics, English, and other subject areas.

Although these dichotomous distinctions might feel neat and tidy in theory, reality tells a different story. The best curriculum and the most professionally prepared teachers in the world cannot reach or teach students who aren't there physically or mentally. Schools across the country are plagued by truancy, absenteeism, dropouts, discipline referrals and suspensions, violence, gangs, drug use, teen pregnancy, and HIV and other sexually transmitted diseases. Underlying factors for these behaviors and conditions in turn point to deficiencies in many of our educational institutions that fail to provide a sense of connectedness to school, healthy adult role models, access to enrichment and extracurricular activities, access to high-quality teachers and instruction, positive reinforcement, opportunities for active involvement for students and their families, and high expectations for all children and youth.

These issues are complex and speak of systemic inequities that are historically based on constructs of race, poverty, power, and privilege. We can no longer afford to expend all our resources on trying to fix the students. We must address the systemic context and conditions of learning to create equity and excellence in our schools across the nation. No school improvement effort can hope to be successful unless these factors are addressed through the creation of a supportive learning environment.

The Need for Action Planning

Conventional wisdom teaches us that a successful endeavor is based on careful planning and methodical implementation. Creating systemic change involves a thoughtful, intentional course of action that pays attention to both the process and the outcome. This book addresses that need by providing easy-to use tools for developing core teams and crafting a solid action plan. The action planning described in this book is designed to create supportive learning environments that improve student performance.

Many books exist on school improvement, yet few of them specifically address the components of the learning environment itself. This book is a template for looking at the myriad issues of the environment that affect student achievement within a well-documented research based framework. The Seven Key

Elements of Supportive Learning Environments document addresses ways to overcome the major barriers to student success. It has broad applicability to a wide variety of behaviors and conditions and will serve as a valuable planning tool for schools and communities looking to improve student success.

How Can this Book Be Used?

The book has been developed as a guide for facilitators and school community teams in developing their own action plans for creating supportive learning communities. The basic premise of any improvement effort is to work smarter, not harder by utilizing existing resources in new and improved ways. Schools and organizations must maintain coherence and cohesion by integrating any new plan into existing plans and initiatives and aligning it with the core goals of improving successful outcomes for youth and their families.

The Action Planning process delineated in this book can best be accomplished through the following venues which currently exist in one form or another in schools and community organizations across the country:

- School Improvement Grants
- No Child Left Behind Mandates
- Closing the Achievement Gap Efforts
- School Improvement Efforts and Student Support Services Coordination
- Home and School Collaborations including Title I Parent Involvement Efforts
- School and Community Collaborations
- Business Apprenticeships
- Community Service and Service Learning Programs
- Mentoring Programs for Youth
- Mentoring Programs for Teachers
- New Teacher Training Programs
- Higher Education Partnerships
- Adult Education Programs

- Small Learning Communities Grants and Initiatives
- 21st Century Community Learning Centers
- After School Advantage Programs
- Extended School Day Programs
- Safe and Drug Free Schools Programs
- Coordinated School Health Programs
- Community and Public Health Initiatives
- Community Based Substance Abuse Prevention Programs
- Dropout Prevention Programs
- Gear Up and College Bound Programs
- Office of Juvenile Justice and Delinquency Prevention Programs
- Foster Care and Family and Children's Services Programs
- Homeless and Runaway Youth Programs including McKinney Funds
- Youth Development Efforts
- Gang and Violence Prevention Programs
- Law Enforcement Collaborations
- Community Revitalization Efforts
- Faith Based Initiatives

The Audience

This book is intended for individuals and professionals working as school administrators, teachers, youth workers, counselors, social workers, adult educators, staff developers, trainers, business and organizational leaders, community organizers, and faith-based leaders who want to transform their schools and organizations into supportive learning communities. Schools, community groups, and faith-based organizations are increasingly charged with developing new initiatives in the field of youth services and student supports. These challenges illustrate the dramatic need of schools and youth agencies to develop a road map for planning the future.

In a time when schools face increasing federal mandates for accountability while being simultaneously confronted with decreasing budgets, issues of collaboration and planning become even more important. A common prerequisite for grant funding is evidence of lasting and sustainable collaborations between schools and community partners. Another concern, particularly at a time of shrinking federal dollars for education, is the need to access resources of schools and communities without relying on external funding.

Many community groups and youth programs are in need of practical and useful materials, training, and technical assistance to implement successful research-based programs for enhancing student learning. In short, any endeavor that seeks to improve the potential for student success and engage the intrinsic competencies and capabilities of our schools and partnering organizations can benefit from the innovative approach contained in this book.

What's In the Book?

This book describes an approach to enhancing student success through the development of supportive learning environments. It aims to improve learning and strengthen organizational capacities through the development of an intentional results-based planning process. The book describes specific strategies for developing and implementing an action plan.

It contains:

- Strategies for creating a diverse school community team
- Techniques and multiple tools for developing a shared vision
- Research-based framework of the Seven Key Elements of Supportive Learning Environments
- Tools and techniques for conducting data-based needs assessment
- Surveys for parents and students
- Community mapping tools
- Change management strategies and tools for prioritizing and sequencing interventions

- Results-based action plan template
- Sample case scenarios and exercises
- Evaluation tools
- Bibliography of resources and references

A Vision of Institutional and Social Transformation

As someone committed to social justice on a personal and professional level, it is my hope that this book can contribute to the ongoing work of social change and transformation within our schools and communities. As educators and people committed to children and youth, we all have the ability to create caring schools and communities that educate all children and provide them equal opportunities to improve their lives.

Meet the Author

Teddy Holtz Frank has a master's degree and certification in social work, and has a postgraduate degree in character analytic therapy. She is president of Health Promotion Associates, Inc., a training and organizational development consulting firm serving public and Fortune 500 clients. Ms. Holtz Frank has authored numerous articles and training curricula and is a contributing author of *Tools for Dropout Prevention,* published by Eye On Education Press. She is currently the Program Coordinator for the Hudson Valley Student Support Services Center.

References

Chisom, R., & Washington, M. (1997). *Undoing racism: A philosophy of international social change.* New Orleans: People's Institute Press.

Delpit, L. (1995). *Other people's children: Cultural conflict in the classroom.* New York: Morrow.

Kohl, H. (1994). *"I won't learn from you" and other thoughts on creative maladjustments.* New York: New Press.

Kozol, J. (1991). *Savage inequalities: Children in America's schools.* New York: Crown Publishers.

Miller, J. B. (1976). *Toward a new psychology of women.* Boston: Beacon Press.

Noguera, P. (2003). *City schools and the American dream.* New York: Teachers College Press.

Payne, Ruby. (1996). *A framework for understanding poverty.* Texas: Highlands, TX: Aha Process.

Tatum, B. (1991). *Why are all the black kids sitting together? And other conversations about race* . New York: BasicBooks.

1

An Overview of the Action Planning Process: How Do We Get to Where We are Going?

Never doubt that a small group of thoughtful committed citizens can change the world: Indeed it's the only thing that ever has.

Margaret Mead

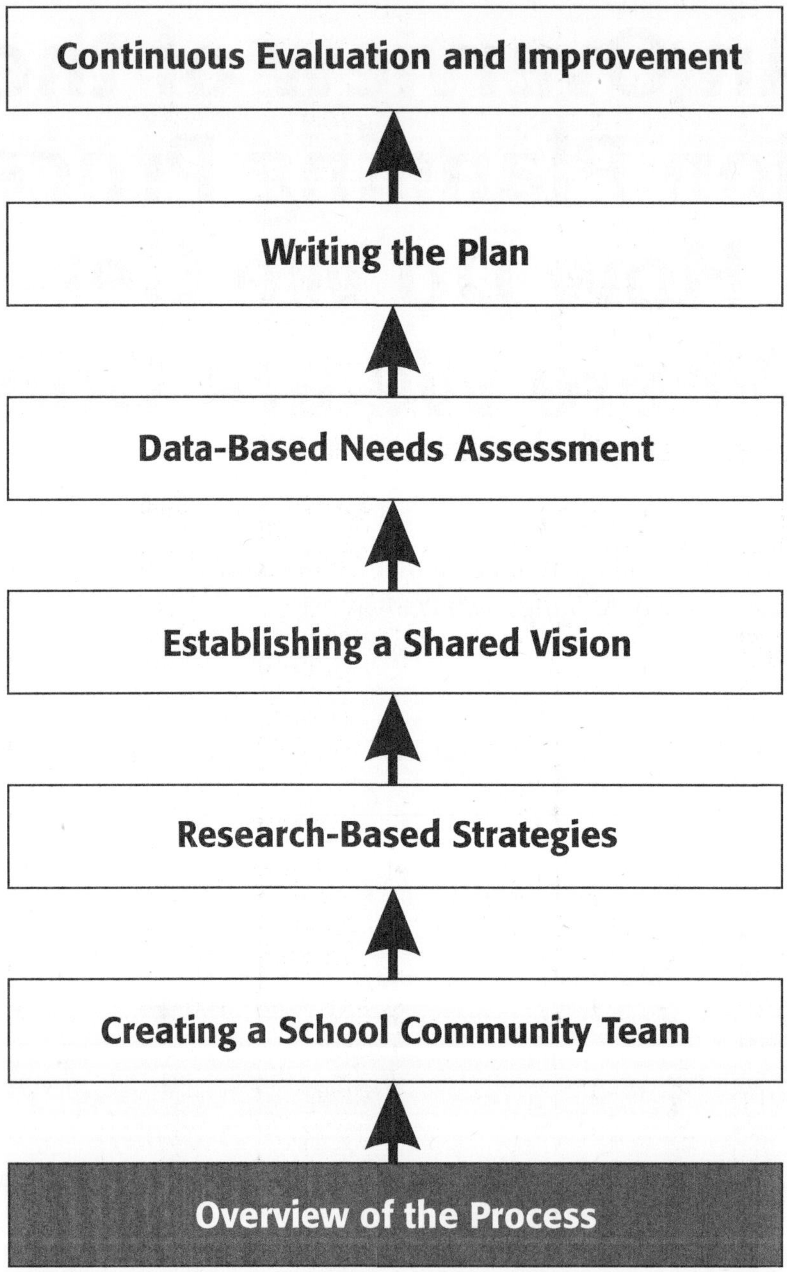
Continuous Evaluation and Improvement
Writing the Plan
Data-Based Needs Assessment
Establishing a Shared Vision
Research-Based Strategies
Creating a School Community Team
Overview of the Process

Focus on the Action Planning, Not the Plan

An action plan is not an end in itself but rather a means to an end. It is essentially a learning process, a living laboratory, research in action. The intentional act of planning forces a team to grapple with a host of questions, including the following: What is our purpose? What do we hope to accomplish? What strengths can we build on? What issue(s) are we addressing? What does the data say about our strengths and areas for improvement? What are the best methods for achieving our aims? What does the research say? How will we know if it's working?

Effective planning builds structures, programs, policies, and practices that create relationships and promote student-centered learning. The end result is less about the document that gets created and more about the results; the systemic changes and the knowledge, skills, and attitude shifts that occur within the school community. The plan is a living, breathing document that needs to be constantly reviewed and refined through ongoing evaluation and continuous improvement processes to stay alive. Otherwise, it becomes one more dead document that gathers dust on the shelf.

General Dwight D. Eisenhower captured this succinctly when he said, "Plans aren't important; planning is!" To paraphrase General Eisenhower, the planning process is what gets things done, not the plan. The plan is a template that will be adjusted and tweaked over time as the team learns from its successes and misses. The action-planning steps outlined in this book, if followed with fidelity, create a smoothly functioning team that is capable of implementing a wide variety of initiatives, all designed to improve student achievement and develop a supportive learning environment.

Guiding Principles of Successful Plans

Many initiatives get started. Few get evaluated for successful outcomes. Even fewer get sustained and embedded into the everyday functioning of the organization. The following principles should guide any effort at systemic improvement:

- The plan is integrated with existing (school improvement and/or strategic) plan to ensure organizational coherence and cohesion.
- The plan is based on a data inquiry process that includes input from multiple data sources and constituents to ensure equitable and diverse representation.
- The plan builds on existing strengths within the organization.
- The plan addresses needs that interfere with learning.
- The plan correlates needs to research-based strategies and/or promising practices to improve fundamental barriers to learning.
- The plan sequences the implementation of strategies for maximum effectiveness.
- The plan assesses the outcomes using supportive evidence.
- The plan shows measurable success in achieving outcomes.

The Action Planning Spiral

Although the steps are laid out sequentially, it is not a linear process. In reality the living plan is more of a spiral that reengages earlier phases at higher and higher levels of functioning (see Figure 1.1). The team constantly evaluates progress along the way and makes course corrections as needed. It is helpful to view this process as a "virtuous teaching cycle" (Tichy & Cardwell, 2002). Team functioning improves, and the individual and collective capacity increase as the team learns to work together. As interventions are implemented, evaluated, and refined, the team gains confidence in its ability to create positive change successfully.

Figure 1.1. The Action Planning Spiral

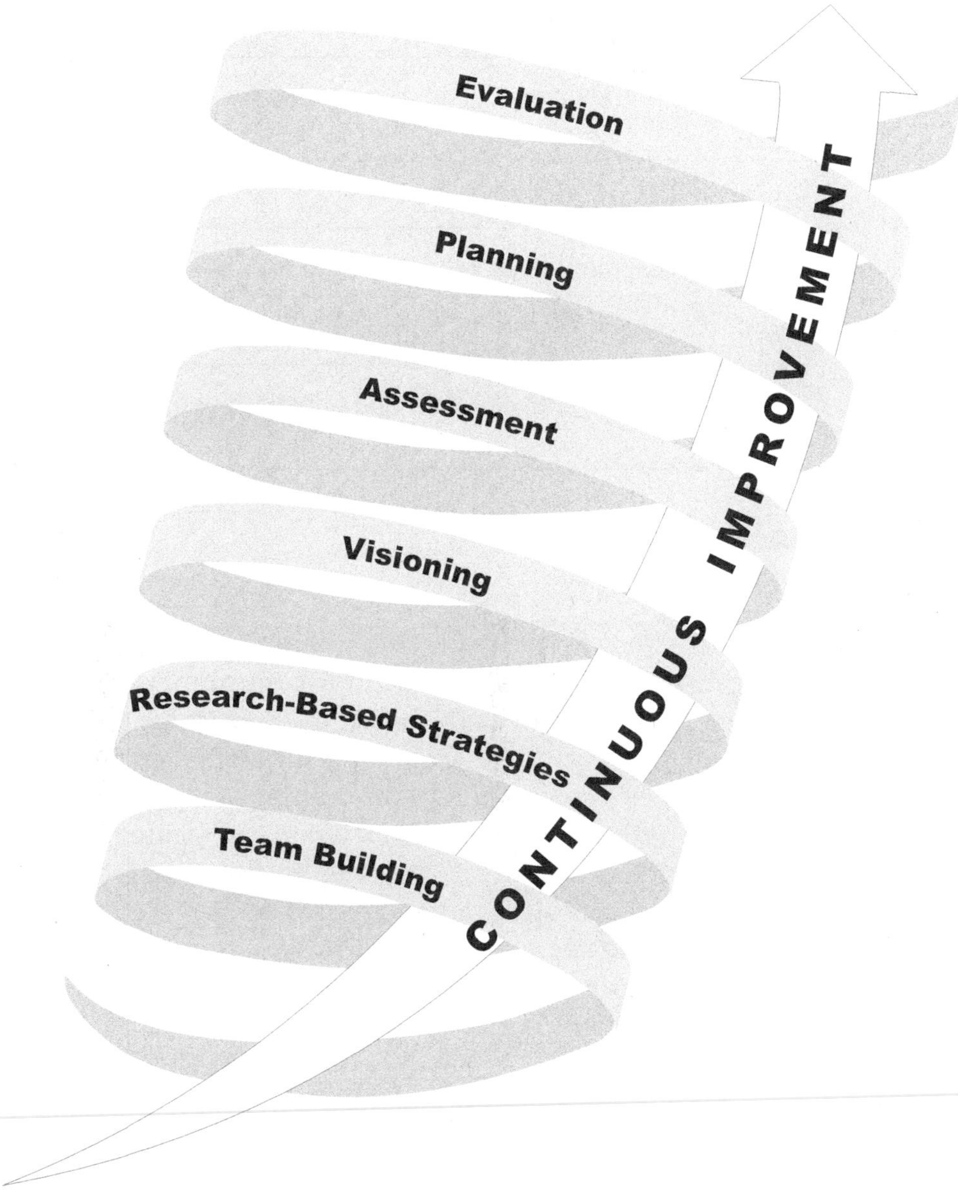

The planning process takes on a life of its own and becomes an opportunity to create a true intentional learning organization. Members learn to rely on mastering the skills of change and improvement rather than on the development of a product. Relationship structures and linkages create shared learning and break down the barriers and isolation of closed systems. This is a hallmark of successful teams, successful leadership, and successful schools and learning environments.

Picture Success: The Steps of the Action Planning Spiral	
1.	Create a diverse, culturally representative school-community team.
2.	Understand the foundation of research-based components of supportive learning environments.
3.	Develop a shared vision and team process.
4.	Conduct a data-based assessment of areas of strength and areas of need.
5.	Write the action plan.
6.	Engage in continuous assessment, evaluation, and improvement throughout every step of the process.

The Steps of the Action Planning Spiral

This book lays out an action planning process that begins with **developing a diverse school community team**. Specific recruitment strategies that are the core of creating diversity are covered in depth in Chapter 2. Innovative techniques for mapping the ecology of the community, methods for assessing and strengthening strategic linkages, and strategies for overcoming resistance are all included in this chapter. Many of these same techniques can be applied to any organizing effort designed to engage diverse representation from the school community or within the student body for broad-based student involvement initiatives.

This team then embarks on a journey of discovery in examining the specific components of environments that create a holistic picture of learning and student supports. **The research foundation of supportive learning environments,** presented in Chapter 3, provides a solid base for understanding and planning student-centered learning communities that enhance student achievement. The research is compiled into the seven key elements of supportive learning environments, which are then further delineated through indicators for success. This model establishes a clear picture, grounded in extensive research, of proven strategies, structures, policies, and practices that are interwoven to form effective and inclusive learner-centered environments.

The team now has a greater understanding of what it is attempting to create and can engage in a deliberate process of **establishing a shared vision**. In Chapter 4 multiple tools are explored in depth to allow members to access the creative brain when developing vision statements. Many of these same strategies can be applied to student learning as well. Sample vision statements from a wide variety of settings and industries are included to expand the conception of what is possible. Additional tools are provided that create structures and protocols for ensuring the safety and trust within the planning team.

Chapter 5 explains a **data-based needs assessment** process that allows the team to engage in reflective, honest discussions about the nature of the successes and areas for improvement within the school community. A conscious, thoughtful exploration of these issues occurs through a finely tuned process that focuses on strengths, builds on existing capacities, and accurately pinpoints areas of need. Predata discussions, based on guiding questions and sample worksheets, are crafted to engage the group in a highly structured design. Team members engage in individual, dyadic, small, and large group sharing of personal observations and hypotheses of causation, surfacing underlying assumptions, and generating questions before jumping to answers and solutions.

Expanding the range of multiple data sources available to the team is a key task for creating informed discussion and decision making. Additional information designed to capture quantitative as well as qualitative data is gathered in a variety of ways in the data collection phase. Sample student and parent surveys, a community resource mapping tool, and a sample checklist of expanded data sources are all included.

Now the team is ready to commit their plan to paper. Chapter 6 provides simple tools for **developing a measurable results-based plan.** Assessing assets and determining gaps helps the group to hone their focus and sequence their change efforts. Establishing priorities and then matching the prioritized needs to selected strategies (using the research-based components of a supportive learning environment form Chapter 3) allows the team to understand the dynamic nature of action planning. Rather than a static plan, this delicate process of matching needs illustrates that there is not always a one-to-one correspondence between problem and solution but rather a series of possible interventions that can address a multitude of areas.

The concept of a dynamic process is further enhanced through the focus on immediate, short- and long-term outcomes. Many of the deeper systemic changes require putting in place the building blocks of smaller incremental steps. This builds in another self-correcting evaluation mechanism for the team. The team can review the results, outcomes, outputs, and indicators to measure progress toward successful implementation. Using these results-based measures allows the team to formulate and sequence its plan incrementally, building on immediate short-term successes to develop the long-term outcomes that lead to lasting and sustainable impacts.

Delineating specific action steps, assigning these tasks to particular individuals, and demarcating timelines helps to clarify roles and responsibilities of team members and ensures progress and momentum in implementing the plan. This is the simplest part of the task because the team has now arrived at the point of readiness for action. The language of results-based planning is alive, active, and easily decipherable, and does not require expending enormous amounts of time and energy in the often-frustrating attempt to create minute, finite measures. Instead, the team can maintain its momentum and excitement as it readies for actual strategy implementation by developing a simple and succinct blueprint for action. The indicators and corresponding evidence of success provide clear and readily accessible tools and benchmarks to measure successful project implementation.

By committing the plan to paper, team members are also deepening their commitment to action. Establishing clarity about what is to be accomplished, how it will be accomplished, and by whom minimizes confusion and dissension in the team. Members know what is expected and can function smoothly together as a team. Individuals are accountable to the team and the plan, which increases buy-in and paves the way toward sustainability of the project.

A common problem that plagues many school improvement efforts is the constant changeover of team members. The lack of stability among people designated as representatives to the team can hamper efforts. By committing the plan to paper, it becomes replicable and ensures greater continuity if members do change. Someone else can step into another person's role and accomplish clearly delineated tasks. Committing the plan to paper helps sustain the project through potential personnel changes and creates a strong infrastructure.

Finally, a **continuous improvement process** allows the plan to become a living document, subject to refinements and revisions based on frequent data-driven assessments of what's working and what's not. Chapter 7 reemphasizes the continuous nature of the improvement process and asks the team to envision the process as a spiraling cycle, revisiting earlier phases and continuing to collect quantitative and qualitative data to inform process and product evaluation. These tools parallel the task of good teaching and learning and become embedded in all aspects of the learning community as a result of the action planning process.

Additional suggestions and tools are incorporated for creating a positive communication and feedback loop to ensure the proper flow of information. Feedback and communication create energy and excitement and are part of the ongoing process of planning and implementation.

Together We Stand, Divided We Fall

Many school administrators may have legitimate concerns about their organizational capacity to embark on a school improvement endeavor. They may be reluctant to undertake an action planning process for fear that it means additional responsibilities for an already overburdened staff. They may feel that their job is to improve the bottom line (test scores) and feel that the myriad issues that affect learning are outside this realm. They may not clearly understand the relationship between student achievement and elements of the learning environment that significantly contribute to student learning such as improving school bonding, school connectedness, student motivation, safety, discipline, classroom management, and community and parent involvement.

The job of educating all students has certainly gotten too big for the school to accomplish alone. Now, more than ever, collaboration and collective effort is called for in improving our schools and our communities. Intentional, well-designed planning and thoughtful implementation are more likely to create sustainable structures and lasting changes that will benefit students and their families.

Reference

Tichy, N. M., & Cardwell, N. (2002). *The cycle of leadership: How great leaders teach their companies to win.* New York: Harper Business.

2

Creating a School/ Community Team: It Takes a Village

I have seen that in any great undertaking it is not enough for a man to depend simply upon himself.

Isna-la-wica (lone Man) Teton Sioux

Individual commitment to a group effort — that is what makes a team work a company work, a society work, a civilization work.

Vince Lombardi

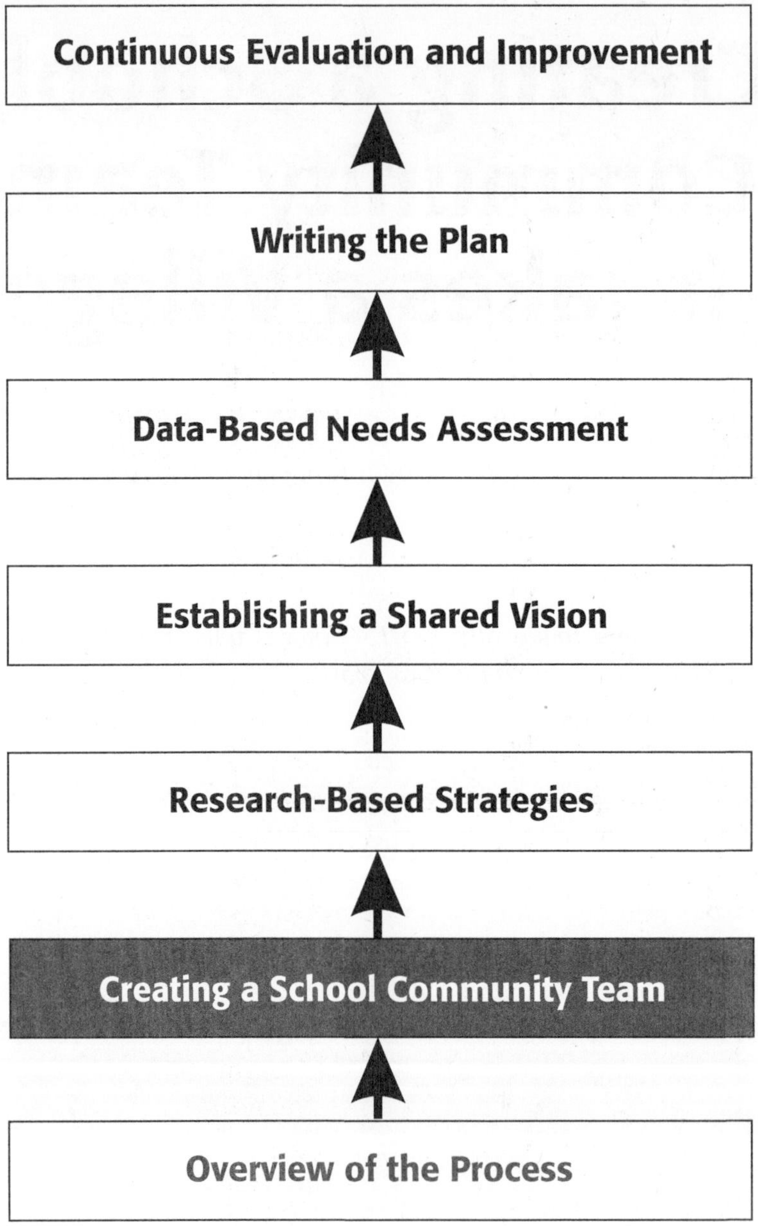

Continuous Evaluation and Improvement
Writing the Plan
Data-Based Needs Assessment
Establishing a Shared Vision
Research-Based Strategies
Creating a School Community Team
Overview of the Process

Picture Success: School Community Collaboration

The Coca-Cola Valued Youth Program, now entering its 20th year, provides peer and cross age tutoring services. Middle school and high school students identified as being at risk of dropping out are paid a stipend to act as tutors for elementary school students. Family involvement is a key component of the program. Started in partnership with Coca Cola, this successful school community collaboration continues to show significant decreases in dropout rates for these high-risk youth: It has increased academic performance, improved communication between schools and families, and renewed family pride (Cardenas, Montecel, Supik, & Harris, 1992).

School/Community Collaborations

The job of having all students successfully graduate from high school is too big to be done by the schools alone. Experience teaches us that no one system can provide the supports necessary to ensure success for all our young people.

Schools bear a special challenge and a unique opportunity. Because of the amount of time a youngster spends in school, it is an ideal setting to form healthy relationships with adults and learn valuable social and academic skills. Yet all too often schools have become places that represent failure for many children. Schools can often be places that alienate or intimidate families and discourage community involvement. Partnering with the community can enhance the assets that help young people succeed.

Assets of Community-Based Programs

There are distinct advantages and assets of youth centers and programs housed in the community. These programs tend to be more culturally responsive to the families within the community. They frequently lend themselves to naturally supportive relationships between adults and young people. Often, the youth workers at these centers are reflective of the cultural makeup of the community and share an understanding of the backgrounds, challenges, and conditions that families and young people face. Community-based programs also have the advantage of not being associated with the rigors and requirements of school—they are often seen as fun places to hang out.

There is a strong case to be made for enrichment as a valuable tool in enhancing social, emotional, and academic learning. The challenge that exists for many of these centers is to become more sophisticated in articulating how their programs significantly affect student learning. This often involves learning how to collect and use data in linking the work they do with student achievement in school.

Increasingly, community partners are seen as allies in the education arena. They may be national agencies such as Big Brothers/Big Sisters, Boys and Girls Club, YMCA, Girl Scouts or Boy Scouts, or local faith-based and social service agencies. These agencies might run afterschool programs, extended day programs, or other types of programs that provide services to families and youth. There is often a lack of congruence and connection between what students do during the school day and at the afterschool youth programs. Although the programs can sometimes take place within the actual school building, many times they are operated by separate youth agencies that function in a totally different context, culture, and climate. There is often the absence of conscious collaboration between these programs and the school.

It takes a concerted effort to establish strong and mutually beneficial connections between schools, youth agencies, businesses, faith-based institutions, and government services. It starts by including all stakeholders at the table from inception. This involves learning the skills of multicultural competence and being willing to share power with all our constituents.

Developing Skills of Multicultural Competence and Power Sharing

Working with multiple partners from varying cultures and backgrounds requires a new set of skills. Private enterprise, over the past several decades, has recognized the importance of dealing with diversity in a global economy. Authors Michael Lombardo and Robert Eichinger (2004) offer the following skill criteria:

Skilled Management of Diversity
▪ Manages all kinds and classes of people equitably ▪ Deals effectively with all races, nationalities, cultures, disabilities, ages, and both sexes ▪ Hires variety and diversity without regard to class ▪ Supports equal and fair treatment and opportunity for all

In the field of human services, this issue has also assumed major importance. The term commonly used, *cultural competence,* has been defined as "an awareness and knowledge of nondominant cultures to more effectively engage clients and families in services." Although this is a valuable start, it assumes no change in the inherent power imbalance between the two parties: service provider and service recipient, or consumer.

Viewed from a different perspective, I prefer to use the term *multicultural competence* and *power sharing,* defined as "the ability to effectively collaborate and remain accountable to one's constituents in a process for mutual growth and improvement, based on a firm commitment to social justice and equity." It is a necessary skill for educators and community professionals dealing with youth and their families in the twentyfirst century.

Multiculturally competent professionals who adhere to power-sharing principles recognize underlying conditions of oppression and address these issues in their practice. To be effective change agents, it is essential that we recognize the impact of poverty, racism, and other institutional barriers to access within the communities we work. Without any analysis of the inherent and ubiquitous power imbalances and inequities, professionals working in poor communities can often create more harm than good through their failure to address the systemic issues that give rise to poverty and racism. Because of either coming from a dominant culture or being an institutional gatekeeper for the dominant point of view, many well-intentioned professionals inadvertently maintain and support inequitable systems of power (Chisom & Washington, 1977). It is not enough to be aware of social injustices and inequalities; we must actively work to change social policies and undo these conditions (North Central Regional Educational Laboratory, 2004; Rothstein, 2004a).

Middle-class assumptions about deficits in achievement, motivation for learning, and patterns of communication can often alienate families who live in poverty or come from another culture or country with different value systems, norms, and expectations. Educators need to become versed in the language and conditions of their students living in poverty if they hope to engage these families and help the students learn and achieve in the school environment (Delpit, 1995; Haberman, 1991; Noguera, 2003; Nieto, 1992; Perry, Steele, & Hilliard, 2003; Rothstein, 2004b).

An underlying prerequisite to achieving a level of multicultural competence and effectiveness as a change agent is to understand as much as possible about the day-to-day conditions faced by families living in the community. How to do this? Ask questions and listen carefully to the descriptions of seemingly simple tasks such as getting medical help; doing the laundry; feeding the family; trying to maintain a regimen of daily hygiene in which hot water and bathing are part of a routine; paying the rent; finding adequate child care, using transportation; being employed; and finding time, space, and quiet for homework and studying.

Listen and acknowledge the realities and corrosive effects of poverty and racism in the lives of youth and their families. Above all, do not pathologize individuals or communities by attributing causes of personal deficiency to these social ills in an attempt to deny or excuse them. This is a subtle and well-practiced form of collusion that gives the message that the professional and the school are unwilling to acknowledge the realities of the students' life. It damages trust, leads to youth and their families filtering information and disconnecting from the school or agency, and severely diminishes the ability to create any effective or lasting change in the lives of young people.

Benefits and Challenges of Creating a Diverse, Equitable Team

Equity refers to the power-sharing principles outlined previously. *Diversity* refers to the inclusion of different types of people working together. Differences include categories of race, ethnicity, culture, gender, socioeconomic status, religion, age, sexual orientation, and ability or disability. The diversity of the team should be culturally reflective and inclusive of the school and community with respect to these differences. Practices of equity and power sharing ensure that all members of the community have equal voices and are represented in their interests and needs.

Diversity presents many opportunities. Learning to leverage diversity within a team enhances the perspectives and possibilities for creative change. Members who might view the world differently from one another are more likely to generate a wider variety of options, ideas, and strategies. People who think alike tend to produce the same kinds of solutions—solutions that might not have been effective in the past. People who think differently are more likely to produce innovation. Effective teams need a mix of experience, expertise, and fresh blood (or new ideas and perspectives).

Practicing diversity and equity presents many challenges as well. It requires a willingness to move beyond one's immediate comfort zone and engage in a critical analysis of power relationships and one's own role in the power arrangement. It also involves educating oneself about the dynamics of race and class in this country and understanding historic constructs that operate to maintain power. It demands a willingness to be nondefensive and open to change and personal transformation.

It requires the development of a strong communication process for resolving differences and conflicts. It requires openness to hearing opinions that might differ markedly from one's own. It demands patience because it takes more time to allow for differing opinions and ideas. Some administrators might be used to making unilateral decisions and then handing them down to be implemented. This type of hierarchical process never allows for true personal investment of the stakeholders, and is one of the core reasons many potentially beneficial initiatives flounder or die.

Engaging Parents from Culturally Diverse Communities

A common complaint echoed by schools is that the families of the students who could most benefit from parental involvement are the hardest to reach. Many school leaders are sincerely perplexed by the issue of engaging parents from poor or immigrant communities and communities of color. These families and communities often have limited access to the dominant power structure that has influence over school board policies and educational practices.

The need to include these traditionally disenfranchised members within our communities is more urgent than ever. Schools are confronted with a widening achievement gap that points to racial and economic disparities between students. The National Task Force on Minority Achievement, points out that "closing the gaps in academic achievement between groups of students from different social divisions (class, ethnicity, gender and language) will require the development of intellective competence in a wide range of individuals through interventions in our homes, communities and schools" (North Central Regional Educational Lab, 2004).

Addressing these racial and economic disparities in achievement requires learning the skills of multicultural competence. It means being open to the inclusion and collaboration of diverse members of our learning community. It also requires a willingness to analyze our schools critically and to correct systemic inequities. This is the art and science of becoming an equitable multicultural institution.

Open recruitment of representatives from communities of color, poor communities, and immigrant communities sends a message that the school is truly committed to educating all children and reaching all families. One of the issues within our dominant institutions is that those in power rarely take the time to listen to their constituents. While giving lip service to diversity, many people in power continue to control the setting, the language, and the structure. As a result, the dialogue is silenced and things remain the same, unequal and ineffective for many of our underrepresented communities.

Inclusion in the process creates buy-in, motivation, and commitment to work together to create a collaborative community of learners. Inclusion also sows the seeds of sustainability because people who have a personal stake in an endeavor will find a way to keep things going after the initial funding and enthusiasm die away. Who has a greater personal stake in creating a learning community and enhancing student achievement than parents do?

Getting parents to join a team or endeavor requires finding out what is important for them, what will cause them to make a personal commitment. Finding out this information involves listening to what people have to say—keeping an ear to the ground. Recruiting poor parents and parents of color can often involve meeting them on their turf, which means going out into the community rather than expecting parents to show up at the school. You might have to bring a translator if the parents speak a language other than English or find someone who has ties in the community to invite a team member to present to a group of parents.

Youth are often the best recruiters of their parents through their persistence and enthusiasm. Parents will often come out to watch their child perform. Parents in turn, are frequently able to engage other parents, often the hardest to reach parents who respond more favorably to someone they know and trust from the community. Parents also often have greater knowledge of the community and can access resources unknown to the school.

Group settings, instead of more traditional one-on-one individual meetings with authority figures, are often more comfortable for many parents of color or poor parents. Informal group settings in which food is served also help to increase the comfort of people who might be intimidated and feel unwelcome in the school. Participating in a more culturally relevant environment within the community also sends the signal that the school is sincere in moving toward a more equitable, diverse, multiculturally competent approach.

Competitive companies functioning in a global marketplace recognize the value of representing their constituents' needs. The perception in a community that the community is culturally responsive can often help the company gain market share (Morrison, 1996). School and organizations can obtain similar benefits by becoming culturally responsive and genuinely enlisting the efforts of diverse parents, youth and community representatives.

Barriers to Establishing a Team

The first obstacle of creating any new initiative or program is the inevitable confrontation with people's fear and unwillingness to change, to challenge the status quo. This challenge involves moving beyond the accepted practices and the familiarity of the in-group, or cluster of individuals who comprise the norm. As human beings, we tend to be afraid of the unknown, the different, and opt to preserve what is most familiar. It can seem like we never really left the junior high school clique—everyone dresses, acts, and thinks alike.

When it comes to establishing a school/community team, schools often ask this question: Why should we go through the challenging process of trying to include other agencies, organizations, or businesses on the team when we are the ones best able to determine the needs of the students? The perception is that these other people or groups are really outsiders and do not understand the way the school must conduct its business. This reluctance to collaborate and reach beyond the school gate is potentially the biggest obstacle that schools face when forming strong and sustainable partnerships with the community.

On the other hand, community-based organizations often feel that the schools are too focused on academics and not focused enough on the social-emotional aspects of children's lives. These organizations often provide children and their families with vital support services such as assistance in housing, medical care, mental health, food, and recreation. These organizations provide a bond between the families and the community, a kind of extended family structure that allows many families to maintain some measure of stability and health.

Too often, the school and the community agencies function in totally separate orbits, as if they are both part of distinct unrelated solar systems. They function with two programs, two sets of staff, and two different cultures. Yet almost all youth-serving agencies in the community share the same population of children as the school.

What is the effect of these disparate cultures on the children and families who interact in both systems? To the extent that there is coordination and cohesion between the school and community, there is proven gain in academic and behavioral progress for students and youth. If there is little or no communication between these entities, an undermining (and even unwitting) collusion can occur that pits one against the other. This results in far less effectiveness at affecting positive change and development for youth. This generally shows up, particularly for our high-risk youth, for whom success in the community does not always translate into academic gains within the classroom.

Unfortunately, there are usually two reasons why these separate entities are motivated to come together. The first is a crisis that shocks the community, such as a youth suicide; a murder in the school or community; or incidents of youth drinking, drugging, or other high-risk behavior. The other reason why people come together is because an external funding source requires evidence of collaboration as a prerequisite to obtaining funding. Regardless of the motivation, getting diverse members of a community to sit down at the table together and have a dialogue is an excellent starting point for creating effective supportive learning environments.

Is It a Group or a Team?

Those of us who were involved in sports teams in our youth can remember the difference between the real team players and the ball hogs (those kids who never passed the ball but tried to take it all the way to the hoop or the finish line by themselves). Even though they may have scored for the team, we somehow resented them and felt they betrayed the very notion of team with their individualistic actions.

We are all part of some organization, school, business, agency, or even family that resembles either a group or a team. What is the difference between a group and a team? And how do we know when we are part of one or the other?

Both groups and teams are composed of more than one individual with separate roles and responsibilities. On the surface, both might look similar because they may appear to be engaged in a common activity. The key difference between the two is that team members are working toward a common goal, whereas a group consists of people working toward different goals. In a group there is limited interdependence; everyone is operating with separate agendas, many of which can be in conflict with each other. Lacking from the group is a unifying vision, philosophy, belief, or outcome that ties one member to another. This kind of group is found in many of our schools, in which teachers work in isolation from one another and from the administration.

A team shares a special bond, a heart, a sense of commitment, loyalty, and an appreciation for collective effort and celebration of joint success. A team is characterized by the combination of interdependence, the reliance on others, and independence—the contribution of our unique talents and skills to the ensemble. The magic of a team is that it enhances and enlarges the ability of individual members. We are more successful with our teammates than we would be on our own.

What ties a team together is engaging in a shared vision and committing to the work of implementing that vision. An adequate communication process needs to be established to resolve differences and move the group forward through the process. Each step of the process needs to be characterized by the same level of inclusion, openness, and commitment to listening and understanding each other in the work of attaining shared goals.

Sometimes we have all felt irritation and impatience with coworkers when we are asked to perform a task together with them. We may have even thought that we'd be better off doing the task by ourselves. We may seek the comfort of working with others who we perceive to be just like us, who share the same point of view. Conversely, even though we may be part of a team, we may avoid working with others and go it solo. These behaviors significantly contribute to many of the problems experienced by groups.

A close look at typical groups or organizations probably reveals one or two core members who shoulder the lion's share of the work. These individuals might experience burnout and resentment, and might wonder why others are not sharing the workload equally. These groups often exhibit the characteristics of insularity, homogeneity, distrust, unwillingness to work with others who are perceived as outsiders, and a lack of openness to change. Clearly, although these are generalizations, organizations that have these characteristics have a greater likelihood of failure and dissolution than a more diverse group.

Successful teams reveal a different picture, however. They have synergy, the complementary merging of different personalities and people. The most successful teams are those that develop the skills to leverage diversity of its members through conscious awareness, recruitment, and development throughout the process.

Creating Working Teams or Subcommittees

District- or school-level improvement teams tend to be large groups, often comprising 25 or 30 members. A group this size is best suited to initial planning and coordination and then periodic review and feedback as the process progresses. The actual work of data collection, strategy implementation, and evaluation is best assigned to smaller units in the form of task groups or subcommittees.

It is generally recommended that task groups range in size from 8 to 12 people. A group this size is like a sailboat, small and fleet (in contrast with a barge, which although capable of carrying a lot of weight, is extremely slow moving). A smaller group (the sailboat) can accomplish tasks and planning with greater efficiency than a large group. A large group (the barge) is important as a community forum for keeping all members involved, providing an overview of progress in planning, and implementing the various phases of the project.

Effective models include forming one large community group (the barge) and then breaking into smaller task groups (the sailboats). Another model is to form an executive or leadership committee in which members are generally chosen through election or consensus. Corresponding subgroups, task groups, or committees that have additional members choose a representative to sit on the leadership or executive committee. This position (which can be held by the same individual, or it can be a rotating position filled by various individuals at different times) serves the function of reciprocal communicator. This individual represents the interests of the subcommittee, shares information with the governing or leadership body on the progress of the task group, and reports to the subcommittee. The representative provides an overview of the entire process and shares any recommendations or new information from the leadership team to the smaller subcommittee.

Either type of structure—an actual leadership team with subcommittees or a large community group with corresponding task groups—allows the inclusion of many people without suffering from the difficulties of having too many people trying to participate in every aspect of the planning team.

However, if the entire team contains fewer than 8 to 12 members, the group might lack energy and might stagnate for lack of fresh ideas. The work invariably falls to the same people, often leading to potential burnout, as mentioned previously. It can still function as a small core group, but it needs to address the issue of recruiting new members immediately. Careful examination of the group's purpose, philosophy, and operating procedures need to be explored if the group is having continuous difficulty attracting new members. Group members should ask the following questions: Are we really interested in opening up to new members? Is our purpose clear or too vague? Are we willing to accept that members might have varying levels of commitment that might be different from our own? They should then be prepared to make an honest assessment. Using the tools described in this chapter can help to form diverse teams whose membership is truly representative of the entire community.

Example: Using the Eco-Map Tool to Establish an Action Team

Let's suppose that your school has proposed a school community collaboration to develop supportive learning environments to improve student achievement. (This process works equally well for seeking funding partnerships to create afterschool programs; for addressing specific issues of dropouts, teen pregnancy, and substance abuse; and for general community mobilization efforts, youth involvement projects, and so on).There is a small core group of people charged with developing a broad-based collaborative effort. Your task is to form an Action Team.

Step 1:

Identify who in the community is affected by the issue—for example, raising student achievement, decreasing teen pregnancy, and so on (see Figure 2.1).

Identify which constituency (there may be more than one) that they represent by using the checklist of suggestions for the potential members of the action team from Figure 2.2. For example, a parent who is a member of a local church or synagogue might also work as a teacher or teacher's aide in the school. In this case, the parent would represent three separate systems on the Eco-Map, all of which are affected by the issue.

Figure 2.1. Ways to Contribute to Youth: Potential Members of the Action Team

Let us look at the various sectors within the community and examine what each might contribute toward promoting the health of young people.

- Parents—Parents are a significant constituency who are often overlooked in the planning process, which can lead to adverse confrontations that often slow down school-related processes for change. Parents are often more than willing to advocate for policies, protocols, services, and programs that enhance the lives of their children. Becoming an ally with parents in an endeavor to build community can help ensure greater cooperation and can create access to the resources that many of these parents bring from their personal and professional lives.
- Youth—Students have their own unique voice and perspective that adds the contemporary and relatable element that is so vital to attracting and retaining this population in youth-related activities and services. Projects and initiatives thought up by adults, regardless of how in tune they may be with young people, cannot compare with the advantage gained by including young people in the process of planning and conceptualizing from the start. Although no one young person can be the spokesperson for the entire group, a core team of youth representatives can add important and critical flavor or elements to the mix that make it youth-centered instead of adult-centered.
- Local Businesses—Area businesses can donate money; supplies such as T-shirts, art materials, equipment, or musical instruments; or resources such as experts who can share their skills and knowledge with young people. They can get involved in career readiness, vocational training, business mentoring, or coaching programs.
- Community-based Organizations—These organizations are tax-exempt, nonprofit, or not-for-profit corporations that provide valuable linkages for young people and their families within the community. They often provide an array of case management services that involve identifying the needs of a family or young person and locating the corresponding resources within the community. Community-based organizations may teach valuable skills, such as mediation, or provide advocacy for families in the social service and criminal justice systems. Many of these organizations are funded through the United Way, religious institutions, private foundations, and grants.
- National Youth Organizations—Organizations such as Boys/Girls Clubs, YMCA/YWCA, Girl/Boy Scouts, Big Brother/Sister, 4-H, and Cooperative Extension programs provide high quality recreational, educational, and mentoring services to youth and their families.

- Social Service Agencies—These agencies are often part of government bureaucracies that provide assistance to families through the Department of Social Services, Child Welfare, and Child Protective Services. They often work in close coordination with related agencies such as Mental Health, Probation, and so on.
- Government Agencies—Youth Bureau, Parks and Recreation, and related municipal organizations provide services to young people through government-funded programs and grants at the county or regional level. Although they are government-funded, they function within the community as service-based organizations, providing recreation, employment opportunities, tutoring, job skills, and case management services. Other government agencies at the state and federal level often fund community-based programs such as the Office of Juvenile Justice and Delinquency Prevention, Substance Abuse Prevention Services, and the Office of Family and Children's Services. Legislation can also make monies available to communities for programs to help homeless families; prevent gang affiliation, teen pregnancy, and substance abuse; and provide job training.
- Legal, Court and Justice System—Family court, probation, legal services corporations, and the criminal justice system provide services to court-involved youth and/or families with resources such as advocacy, legal representation, and case management. They may also offer skill-building classes in anger management, job readiness, parenting, and medical or mental health services.
- Higher Education—Universities and community colleges can often provide student interns or research and evaluation services for programs that service young people and their families. Student volunteers can provide valuable services—at no cost to the school—through supervised internships in exchange for college credits.
- Faith-Based Organizations—Many faith-based organizations operate community centers as part of their religious instruction or as an adjunct to their services. These organizations can often provide valuable assets to youth programming such as existing programs, space, personnel, and access to families. Many also provide vital services such as food banks, clothing, and so on.
- Medical and Mental Health Agencies—Hospitals, community medical centers, community mental health centers, and individual medical practitioners can provide services to families as well as access for youth programming. They might function as mentors; expose young people to the variety of careers in the medical field; and even assist in the health education components such as drug and alcohol prevention, and HIV/AIDS, STDs, and pregnancy prevention.

Figure 2.2. Checklist of Partners to Include on a School-Community Team

_____ Parents

_____ Youth

_____ Public Schools: High School, Middle School, Elementary School

_____ Private and Nonpublic Schools

_____ Preschool Programs

_____ Adult Education Programs

_____ Community-based Organizations Serving Youth and Families

_____ National Youth Organizations

_____ Government Organizations Serving Families and Youth

_____ Social Service Agencies

_____ Court and Judicial System

_____ Law Enforcement

_____ Medical Services

_____ Mental Health Agencies

_____ Faith-based Organizations

_____ Local Businesses

_____ Civic Clubs and Organizations

_____ Recreation and Athletic Programs

_____ Senior Citizens' Services

_____ Volunteer Organizations

_____ Libraries

_____ Universities and Community Colleges

_____ Sororities and Fraternal Organizations

_____ Transportation Systems

_____ Entertainment & Arts Programs

_____ Corporations housed in the Community

Create separate circles for "Elementary School", "Middle School," and "High School" instead of using one big circle marked "School"; or write "Youth Bridge," Kid's Place," and so on in separate circles to denote specific community programs rather than using one generic circle marked "Community Based Organization." You can have many circles on the page.

Step 2:

Using the Community Eco-Map shown in Figure 2.3, designate separate circles for each individual system and denote any existing contacts within those systems.

Write the name and the role of anyone within the system who is currently involved in the school. For example, write "Mary Biggs, social worker" inside the "Kid's Place" circle. There might be several members designated within the same circle (e.g., the "High School" might be represented by a district level administrator such as the Director of Pupil Personnel or Mathematics, a guidance counselor, a coach, and a biology teacher.

Use a solid line (_____) to denote a strong or solid connection to the team.

Step 3:

Draw a line between the Action Team in the center of the Eco-Map and each of these circles, designating the nature of their connection.

Use a dotted line (————-) to denote a tenuous connection to the team. For example, a middle school principal might have been told by the superintendent to participate but might not be on board fully, or a community agency might be running a youth mediation program for students in the school but might have no real connection to the school.

Use a railroad line (/\/\/\/\/\) to denote a problematic or adversarial connection. For example, a particular teacher within the school might be very negative toward any additional work or projects and may actively try to block the efforts of the team, or the executive director of an influential community-based agency does not think the schools know anything about running an afterschool program and has been unwilling to collaborate in the past.

Figure 2.3. Community Eco-Map

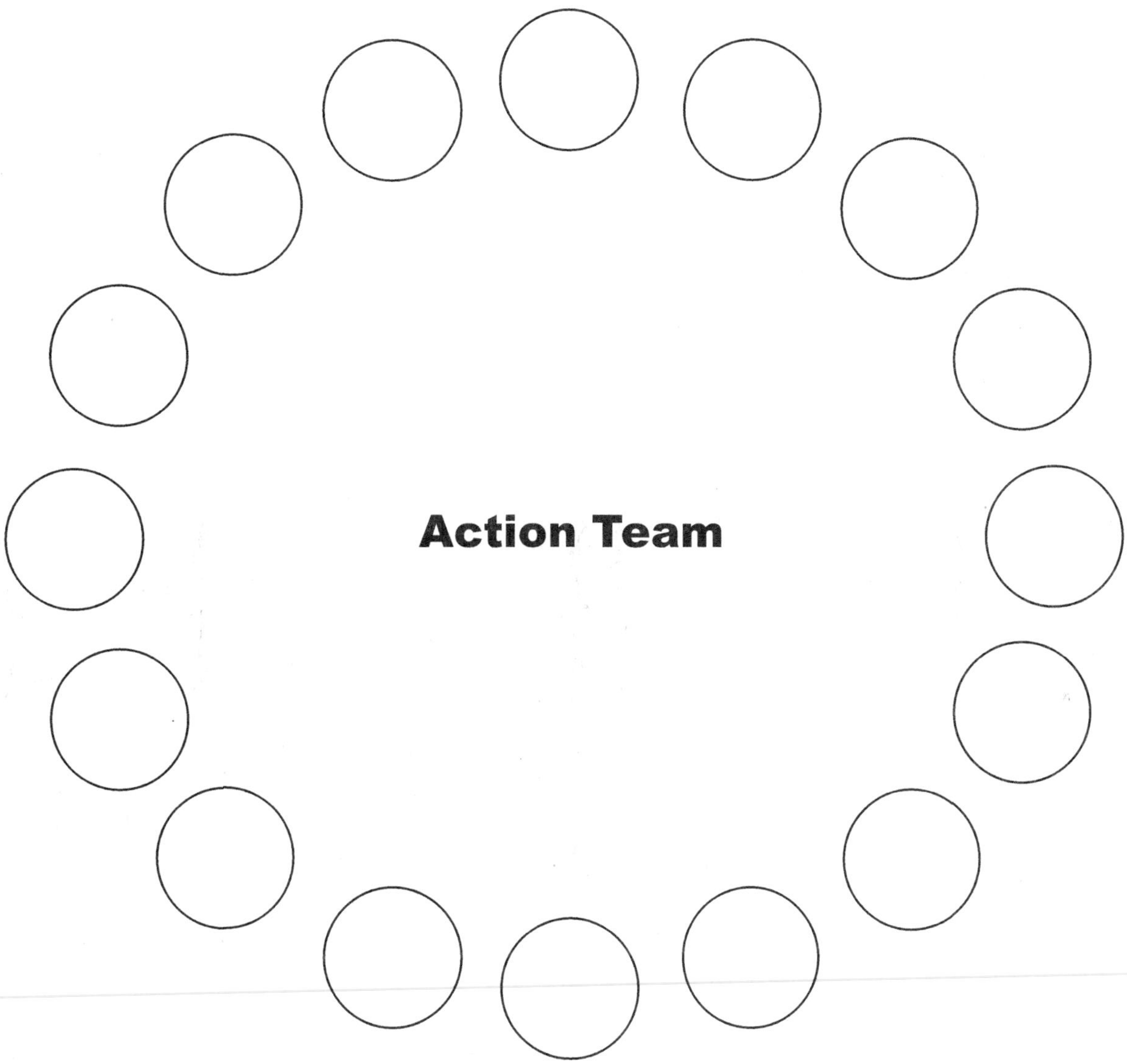

Mark the name of the various organizations and systems within your community. Refer to the list in Figure 2.1.

______ = strong, solid connection
_ _ _ _ = tenuous or weak connection
/\/\/\/\ = problematic or adversarial connection

Step 4:

Identify each system that should be represented but is not currently involved with the school.

Draw a separate circle with the name of the system ("Court System," "Business," "Community," and so on). Draw a broken line (- - -) from the Action Team in the center, connecting any of these groups. Write "To be established" above the line to denote that this is not simply a tenuous connection, as is normally denoted by a broken line.

Step 5:

Identify a specific member within each system who can be contacted by the Action Team and write their name in the circle.

If no one in the group is known, assign that task to a member of the team to establish a contact and connection.

Step 6:

Designate who might be the best person from the Action Team to contact each specific member of the groups or systems listed on the Community Eco-Map and write the name above the dotted line.

Discuss who would be the person within the core group most likely to positively influence this system by factoring in a prior relationship or connection, a similarity of position or background, or an ability to communicate favorably.

The same process can occur for the adversarial or problematic line (denoted by railroad lines—/\/\/\) by assigning the task to a group member to try and improve the relationship using the WIFM (What's In It for Me?) method to gain buy-in (see the following section).

Keep in mind the notion of WIFM, and look at it from the point of view of how involvement in the project can benefit the system.

Use the WIFM Method to Recruit a Diverse Team

Using the WIFM method involves literally "tuning in" to the radio station or frequency from which the group or individual operates. I refer to this process as WIFM (What's In It for Me). See Figure 2.4 for a sample WIFM strategy worksheet.

- Identify the Problem

  List the specific ways in which the problem you are addressing may affect this particular individual, system, or organization.
- Personalize the Benefits

  Listen to find out what the personalized benefits are that the individual or organization is looking for by being involved in your school community team. This focus keeps the needs of the individual or organization foremost and addresses WIFM, which is realistically what most people consider when making a decision.
- Tailor the Answer

  By listening closely, then answering that question effectively and tailoring the answer to the specific needs of the individual or group, many of the barriers to change can be overcome.
- Anticipate Concerns

  Prior to engaging with the individual or system, ask the group to anticipate potential areas of concern that might be posed by the individual or organization within the community.
- Determine Potential Gains

  Equally important is the need for the group to determine what potential gains the prospective system can garner from its involvement. The team must be prepared with a host of personalized reasons for being involved. Although no one wants to be involved in a project that represents lots of work with little gain, many people want to be involved in something that generates valuable commodities—such as recognition and respect, positive public relations, training or staff development, access to resources, improvement in the community, civic pride, and even associated financial gain.
- Understand That Positives Need to Outweigh Negatives

  Like any good sales strategy, the group must provide compelling reasons why the positive aspects of involvement outweigh the negative aspects.
- Prepare Counterarguments

  Like any good debater or politician, the group must be prepared with counterarguments that illustrate both the collective as well as the individual gain that involvement in the team effort can provide for each particular system.

Figure 2.4. WIFM Strategy Worksheet

System	Areas of Concern	Benefits of Involvement

Example: Using the WIFM Method

Using the Eco-Map Tool and process described previously, the group has identified a local photography business as a potential member of the Action Team. You want to ask the owner to get involved as a representative of the business sector.

Examples of these concerns might include high employee turnover, difficulty finding and retaining qualified labor (which results in lost revenue), the high cost of advertising to attract new business, competition with other similar businesses, or trying to ensure customer loyalty in a competitive market.

Step 1:

Brainstorm a list of problems or areas of concern that the photography shop might face when doing business in the community.

Arguments for prospective benefits might include the following: Higher academic achievement creates a pool of more qualified workers; an improved work ethic and greater sense of responsibility create better retention of workers, which saves money on recruitment and training; high visibility in the community creates free advertising to a potential pool of families who could become customers; and civic service to the schools creates greater customer loyalty.

Step 2:

Brainstorm a list of potential benefits from involvement on your school community team that might address the business' concerns.

Have a counterargument for any perceived disadvantages that the business owner might come up with in terms of spending time, money, or energy on your school improvement effort. Reemphasize the benefits that most closely align with the owner's needs. For example, if the individual cites growing competition, emphasize the large potential customer pool. Include actual numbers of families in the school with questions such as this: Did you know we have more than 2000 families who attend public schools in our district, and that number is growing rapidly?

Step 3:

Be prepared to listen and anticipate any concerns about becoming involved. Respectfully show how the benefits outweigh any presumed disadvantages.

Area of Concern	Benefit of Involvement
High employee turnover	Higher retention
Lost revenue	Greater revenue
Difficulty finding skilled labor	More-skilled workforce
High cost of advertising to attract new customers	Pool of potential customers of families who need service
Difficulty retaining customer base	Customer loyalty

References

Cardenas, J. A., Montecel, M. R., Supik, J. D., & Harris, R. J. (1992). The Coca-Cola Valued Youth Program: Dropout prevention strategies for at-risk students. *Texas Researcher, 3,* 111–130.

Chisom, R., & Washington, M. (1997). *Undoing racism: A philosophy of international social change.* New Orleans: People's Institute Press.

Delpit, L. (1995). *Other people's children: Cultural conflict in the classroom.* New York: Morrow.

Haberman, M. (1991). The pedagogy of poverty versus good teaching. *Phi Delta Kappan, 73*(4), 290–294.

Lombardo, M. M., & Eichinger, R. W. (2004). *FYI for your improvement: A guide for development and coaching,* 4th ed. Minneapolis: Lominger.

Morrison, A. M. (1996). *The new leader: Leadership diversity in America.* San Francisco: Jossey-Bass, Inc.

Nieto, S. (1992). *Affirming diversity: The socio-political context of multicultural education.* New York: Longman.

Noguera, P. (2003). *City schools and the American dream.* New York: Teachers College Press.

North Central Regional Educational Laboratory. (2004). *All students reaching the top: Strategies for closing academic achievement gaps.* Naperville, IL: Learning Point Associates.

Perry, T., Steele, C., & Hilliard III, A. (2003). *Young, gifted and black.* Boston: Beacon Press.

Rothstein, R. (2004a). *Class and schools: Using social, economic, and educational reform to close the black-white achievement gap.* New York: Economic Policy Institute and Teachers College, Columbia University

Rothstein, R. (2004b, October). Class and the classroom. *American School Board Journal,* 17–21.

3

Examining Research-Based Elements of Supportive Learning Environments: Building the Foundation

Our goal in developing supportive learning environments is to increase student achievement and successful outcomes for youth in all domains: intellectual, emotional, social, spiritual, and academic.

Continuous Evaluation and Improvement
Writing the Plan
Data-Based Needs Assessment
Establishing a Shared Vision
Research-Based Strategies
Creating a School Community Team
Overview of the Process

Element 1:	Safety of the Physical Plant
Element 2:	Shared Leadership Practices
Element 3:	Structured Personalized Learning Communities
Element 4:	Student Centered Learning Practices
Element 5:	Caring Relationships and Sense of Community
Element 6:	Schoolwide Positive Discipline and Self-Management Practices
Element 7:	Active Student, Staff, Family, and Community Involvement

This chapter describes the seven key elements (see Figures 3.2 to 3.8 pages 65–77) of supportive learning environments. These seven key elements, as well as the indicators for success, derive from an extensive review of the research that explores key components of environments that support student learning and achievement. There are many overlapping variables and elements throughout the literature on supportive learning environments. Although there is no one template, the seven key elements proposed here attempt to synthesize these components into a cohesive whole that schools and youth organizations can use for devising quality programs and learning communities.

In addition, I have pulled from foundational research in the related fields of *resiliency*(Benard, 1997; Rutter, 1987; Werner & Smith, 1982, 1992), *youth development* (Catalano, Berglund, Ryan, Lonczak, & Hawkins, 2002; Pittman & Milgram, 1996; Pittman, O'Brien, & Kimball, 1993), *social learning theory and related effective programs* (Bandura, 1977; Battistich, Schaps, Watson, & Solomon, 1996; Botvin, 1983; Botvin, Baker, Dusenbury, Tortu, & Botvin, 1990; Ellickson & Bell, 1990; Schinke, Botvin, Trimble, Orlandi, Gilchrist, & Loclear, 1988; Schinke, 1999), *effective leadership practices* (Bennis & Goldsmith, 1997; Covey, 1989; Elmore, 2000; Waters, Marzano, & McNulty, 2003), *systems change* (Senge, 1990), *appreciative inquiry* (Cooperrider, Whitney, & Stavros, 2003), and *emotional intelligence* (Csikszentmihalyi, 1996; Gardner, 1993; Goleman, 1995; Seligman, 1990).

The Seven Key Elements of Supportive Learning Environments

These elements should be viewed as a whole, synergistically working together to create a total environment. The action planning process described in this book allows schools to make accurate, data-based decisions about which elements are currently in place, which elements need strengthening, and where critical gaps exist. Schools are not expected to create the whole cloth from scratch, but each school or learning environment has strengths, assets, and existing elements that can be reinforced to create a fuller and more-supportive environment.

The individual components themselves significantly overlap. For example, school safety begins with the physical plant, but is affected in large measure by the quality of the relationships. Many of the student-centered learning practices are also part of the structures that create personalized learning environments. The issue of high expectations for all children and inclusion of all members of the community relate to multicultural competence, parent and community involvement, youth participation, and classroom instruction and assessment.

View these separate components as spokes in a wheel, bricks in a foundation wall, or colors in a rainbow spectrum that together create the structure of supportive learning environments (see Figure 3.1, page).

Element 1: Safety of the Physical Plant

Although safety has always been a major concern for schools, recent events such as the Columbine school massacre (April 1999) and the attacks on the World Trade Center and the Pentagon on 9/11 have thrust it back into the spotlight. Legislation passed by many states now strictly regulates the planning and implementation of school safety. Although variations exist from state to state, the physical requirements for safety in schools are the same.

Safety is a major factor for students in measuring whether they feel connected and satisfied with the overall school environment (Resnick, Bearman, Blum, Bauman, Harris, Jones,

Tabor, Beuhring, Sieving, Shew, Ireland, Bearinger, & Udry, 1997). Of course, many of the most important elements of school safety—such as a safe and supportive climate, trusting relationships with adults, equitable discipline policies, and antibullying programs (Schneider, Walker, & Sprague, 2000)—fall outside the parameters of the physical plant. Although they are clearly elements of supportive learning environments, there must be a priority for establishing an adequate planning process to ensure the physical safety of the students and adults in the building.

Schools must create planning teams to deal with all aspects of safety, including crisis and emergency preparedness. These teams can use the same concepts described in Chapter 2 to form representative teams of youth, parents, and community members. Teams must view their plans as living documents, periodically assessing and revising their plans as needed.

One of the most effective tools for safety planning and emergency preparedness is the use of tabletop exercises, which provide an opportunity to practice managing school emergencies in a simulated situation. Often conducted as part of half-day or whole-day staff development sessions for the entire safety team, the tabletop activities engage participants in assessing and resolving problems in a sample scenario. Discussions about the clarity and effectiveness of safety procedures in resolving these sample emergencies help refine existing plans.

Successful school safety planning requires ownership and specific tailoring of the plan to meet the needs of the school community. Many excellent resources exist for guiding this actual safety planning process (Jalloh & Fuchs Nadeau, 2000; Drug Strategies, 1998; U.S. Departments of Education and Justice, 2000). Recently, the U.S. Department of Education has created new web resources to help school/community teams in the planning process. The FBI Threat Assessment Guide provides clear guidelines for situations involving potential targeted violence (Fein, Vossekuil, Pollack, Borum, Modzeleski, & Reddy, 2002).

Web Resources

U.S. Department of Education

Emergency Planning, Office of Safe and Drug-Free Schools
http://www.ed.gov/emergencyplan

FBI Threat Assessment Guide
http://www.ed.gov/offices/OESE/SDFS

Element 2: Shared Leadership Practices

Picture Success: Outstanding Principals

Journalist Samuel Casey Carter interviewed more than 100 principals from high-performing, high-poverty schools in which at least 75% of the students come from low-income families but score in the top one-third on national exams. He provided a compelling description of effective principals: "Outstanding principals know that all children can excel academically regardless of race, income level, or family background. Studying their success should be the highest priority of educators in a country where more than half of all low-income fourth-graders cannot even read."

Discussing a few of the common traits he found among these principals, Carter said, "Achievement is the key to discipline...Schools must teach by example that self-control, self-reliance, and self-esteem—all anchored in achievement—are the means to success. Success, in turn, inspires confidence, order, and discipline in students."

"Principals work with parents to make the home a center of learning. A lack of parental involvement is often the first excuse for poor performance. Effective principals overcome this by extending the mission of the school into the home. They establish contracts with parents to support their child's efforts to learn. These principals harness a parent's support and motivation by teaching parents to read to their children and check homework."

"Effort creates ability. Good principals demand that their students work hard. Long days, extended years, afterschool programs, weekend programs, and summer school are all features of outstanding schools. Effective principals eliminate social promotion. Students must fulfill specific course requirements to advance. No student is promoted without a clear demonstration of mastery."

Carter concluded by stating, "Nothing I've described is beyond the reach of any school in America. But if we are to see more such schools, we need to stop making excuses for failure."

("Poor children can learn: Successful inner-city schools share common traits." *Chicago Tribune,* June 17, 1999)

Leader as teacher is not about "teaching" people how to achieve their vision. It is about fostering learning for everyone.

Peter Senge

Walk into a building of any school and you immediately get a sense of the personality and style of its leader. Observe the interaction between students, faculty, and visitors. Go into the front office, a classroom, the hallways, and the cafeteria. In each location, ask these questions: Is this a place I want to work? Is this a school I want my child to attend? Are people alive, energetic, and engaged? And most importantly, is learning taking place?

Effective schools are essentially learning communities (Sergiovanni, 1994). Effective leaders create an environment that encourages learning and teaching to occur at every level of the organization until the entire school becomes engaged in a "virtuous teaching cycle" (Tichy, 2002). True engagement in teaching and learning increases the competence and performance of all members of the school community from faculty and administrators to students and families. This fosters a greater sense of personal responsibility, self-management, commitment, and accountability.

High-performing schools bear the hallmark of an active and effective leader who models the way through aligning behavior with a deep and abiding sense of personal ethics (Bennis & Goldsmith, 1997; Covey, 1989; Kouzes & Posner, 2002). Effective leaders begin with a vision for change and improvement. They engage in constant communication of this vision until it binds people together in a common sense of purpose and a shared vision of the possible future. They have a willingness to persist in the face of obstacles and confront reality head-on. They recognize that their job is to build leadership throughout the organization by encouraging critical thinking and structuring leadership opportunities for all members.

The essence of this leadership style is far from the archetypal charismatic general acting as lone hero. Instead, the new leader of the 21st century keeps the organization's attention and focus on the work of "deep restructuring" (Hilliard, 1991; Elmore, 2000) and "second order change" (Waters, Marzano, & McNulty, 2003) rather than on short-term fixes or feel-good solutions. The 21st century school is characterized by authentic involvement and collaboration at all levels of the organization and a sense of shared responsibility. Perhaps most telling of all, effective leaders accept personal responsibility for the success of their students. Their motto may well be this: Failure is not an option.

Web Resources
Center for Creative Leadership http://www.ccl.org
American Association of University Women: Promoting equity in education for girls and women http://www.aauw.org
Center for Leadership and Learning Communities http://cllc.edc.org

Element 3: Structured Personalized Learning Communities

Years ago, I worked as a visiting artist at the Park East School, as it was affectionately called, located in East Harlem, New York City. I performed interactive music from around the world and engaged students in songwriting and instrument building. I can still recall the level of energy and excitement that the students had about learning and the strong feeling of school as community. This school, founded by Deborah Meier, has served as a model to many other schools across the country that try to personalize their own environments.

Picture Success: One Small School in Harlem

In 1974, Deborah Meier founded Central Park East Secondary School, an alternative public school in East Harlem. The school achieved national recognition for its success: More than 90% of Central Park East's students graduate, and more than 90% of those graduates go on to college (in a city where, on average, only 50% of all public school students even graduate from high school). Some of Deborah Meier's innovative approaches included longer class periods (up to two hours), teachers addressed by their first names, interdisciplinary learning in small groups, active inquiry and student participation in classes, a curriculum that relates real life to learning (such as mapping Manhattan or testing the water quality in the East River), and student assessments that include public exhibitions to demonstrate students' learning. In her words: "Every child is entitled to be in a school small enough that he or she can be known by name to every faculty member in the school and well known by at least a few of them, a school so small that family can easily come in and see the responsible adults and the responsible adults can easily and quickly see each other. What size is that exactly? It can't be too small, but surely it can't be larger than a few hundred!" (Meier, 1995, p. 117)

Web Resource

Bill & Melinda Gates Foundation
Valuable resources on small schools and personalized learning environments
http://www.gatesfoundation.org/default.htm

An Antidote to Alienation

Much has been said about the feeling of alienation and anomie that surrounds life in the big cities, big schools, and technological environment of the 21st century. Although no one is suggesting turning back the clock to the days of one-room schoolhouses, there is evidence that consistently supports the restructuring of large schools into smaller schools, classes, or teams (Allen & Steinberg, 2004; Cotton, 1998; Lee & Smith, 1997; National Association of Secondary School Principals, 2004; Seidman, Aber, Allen, & French, 1996; U.S. Department of Education, 1999; Wasley, 2000).

These smaller structures create more personalized units of learning and employ many of the concepts discussed in Element 4 and Element 5: mentoring practices, transition programs, and advisory programs.

What these elements or structures all have in common is the concept that every child needs significant relationships with adults to learn and develop (Benson, Scales, Leffert, & Roehlkepartain, 1999). The essence of these programs is the rich web of connections that tie the students and their families to the schools and the strong sense of community that exists, as described so eloquently by Debra Meier.

Programs and Practices

Promising practices for personalizing school environments that have been proven effective for increasing student achievement and reducing dropouts include advisory programs (Education Alliance, 2003; National Middle School Association, 2001), mentoring programs (LoSciuto, Rajala, Townsend, & Taylor, 1996; Tierney, Grossman, & Resch, 1995), transition programs (Adelman & Taylor, 2002; Eccles, Wigfield, Midgley, Reuman, Mac Iver, & Feldlaufer, 1993; Mac Iver, 1990; Schumacher, 1998), schools within schools (Oakes & Guiton, 1995), and looping (National Association of Secondary School Principals, 2004).

Providing a continuum of intervention services and supports (Dryfoos, 1998; Holtz Frank, 1996), including counseling and alternative placement if necessary, are additional practices that strengthen connections between students, families, community and school.

Mentoring Programs

Picture Success
The Daniel Webster Project at California State University at Fullerton uses the expertise and guidance of the college debate team to teach debate skills to public school students who have been identified as being at risk of dropping out. Successful results of this program indicate an increase in student engagement and commitment to staying in school.

Mentoring programs generally pair a student with a carefully matched mentor to engage in quality relationships for a period of time. Mentors can be an older student, an adult, or a senior citizen in the case of cross-generational programs. These programs traditionally find that the relationship helps both students and mentors, and that students experience gains in self-esteem, learn valuable social skills, and have increased academic aspirations and performance.

There are many excellent resources for mentoring that contain extensive searchable online databases of local mentoring programs—as well as references and training materials on the selection, recruitment, training, supervision, and evaluation involved in successful programs.

Web Resources
The National Mentoring Partnership http://www.mentoring.org
The National Mentoring Center http://www.nwrel.org/mentoring

Advisory Programs

Although much has been written about advisory programs, there is no one model that fits all. The purpose is essentially to have each student known by at least one adult. The actual structure of the program generally has an adult—such as a teacher, administrator, or other staff member—who acts as advisor to a particular student or group of students, usually no more than 20. These advisories can happen individually or in a group, as part of homeroom or classroom session, or at another regularly scheduled time.

Many adults balk at the concept of being an advisor, equating that with being a counselor or mental health specialist. In fact, the activities conducted by the advisor are closer to the role of facilitator, mentor, and teacher, although training is generally recommended for staff members who act as advisors. Listening skills, communication skills, interacting with other staff and parents, and maintaining appropriate boundaries within the relationship are all aspects of being an effective advisor.

Advisors may spend time with students "discussing problems with individual students, giving career information and guidance, developing student self-confidence and leadership, and discussing academic issues, personal or family problems, social relationships, peer groups, health issues, moral or ethical issues and multicultural issues/intergroup relations" (Mac Iver, 1990, p. 459). Additionally, linkages with the community to engage in service learning projects can be a significant activity of advisory groups (see Element 4, page 50).

The benefits of advisory programs include improving peer relationships and relationships between students and adults; increasing school connectedness and engagement; and, when combined with service learning, fostering civic responsibility and increasing motivation for learning. Teachers and parents also experience benefits from advisories because these programs contribute to the sense of community experienced by all members of the school.

Web Resources
Educators for Social Responsibility http://www.esrnational.org/me/reform/msadvisory.htm
National Middle School Association http://www.nmsa.org http://www.nmsa.org/research/ressum9.htm
Middleweb: Exploring School Reform http://www.middleweb.com/advisory.html
The Education Alliance at Brown University http://www.alliance.brown.edu/pubs/changing_systems/power_of_advisories/index.shtml

Transition Programs

Schools that examine their data often find that the preponderance of discipline issues, risk behaviors, and low achievement occur during the last year of middle school and the first year of high school. These issues point to the need for transition programs for students who are changing schools. Particularly vulnerable are the early adolescents, aged 11–14, who are usually the ones moving from an elementary school, in which they may have known everyone, to a large and somewhat impersonal middle school. Even more dramatic is the shift from middle school to high school with its accompanying greater sense of freedom and responsibility. This sudden entry into a building that is often larger, scarier, and full of new and challenging experiences can be very intimidating for many students who may not be prepared to deal with the autonomy and demands of their new environment.

Transition programs are designed to ease the transitions from one school to another. Some of the techniques used include buddy programs (students are paired with older students), student and family orientation sessions, welcome centers, information centers, and advisory programs.

Web Resources

UCLA School Mental Health Project
Center for Mental Health in Schools
http://www.smhp.psych.ucla.edu

(Follow the links for Search and use the drop-down menu for Transition Programs.)

Looping

Picture Success: Looping Program

"Langley Park-McCormick Elementary in Hyattsville, Maryland, is an inner-city school overcoming the odds of some daunting demographics. It is doing this, in part, through a program of looping. Students there are achieving in spite of the problems inherent in their diversity—many cultures (37 countries), multiple languages (25), high poverty, homelessness, and lack of formal education among parents. At the Langley School, which serves grades four through six, educators are using the stability of looping to connect with students and to show a caring attitude. Looping, along with incentives for attendance and exhibiting/highlighting students' work, have helped Langley students find greater success." (Denault, 1999, p. 21)

Another practice that has shown promise in learning social skills and improving relationships between students and peers, students and teachers, and teachers and parents is known as looping, in which a teacher remains with the same class for two or more grade levels.

This practice is more common at the elementary level. Different innovative models are being explored at the middle school and high school levels, where looping can be combined with the concept of advisory groups in the sense that students are divided into grade-level teams and assigned to some of the same teachers for two or more years.

Web Resources
School Redesign Network at Stanford University http://www.schoolredesign.net (Use the Search function to find numerous resources on looping.)

Afterschool and Out of School Time Programs

Afterschool and extended day programs are extremely valuable components of supportive learning environments (refer to Chapter 2). When operated well, they are prime examples of school-community collaborations and attest to how these partnerships and quality programs can enhance student achievement and create a true community of learners.

Successful evaluation results show that students who participated in afterschool programs had better school attendance; performed better on standardized tests in reading, language arts, and math; and were more likely to be reclassified as English-proficient than their nonparticipating peers. In addition, participants increased their grade point averages and showed improvement in school attendance and study skills (Schinke, 1999; U.S. Dept. of Ed., 2003).

Quality afterschool programs and extended day programs can take place before or after school, on weekends, on vacations and holidays, and during the summer recess. It is imperative that these programs maintain a strong connection with what students are doing during the school day, so there has to be direct communication with teachers about the students' schoolwork, homework, and current areas of strength or areas in need of improvement. This kind of personalized assistance can often make the difference for students between failing and passing.

Although there is no one model, programs that occur outside of school time need to keep a strong focus on youth development, including young people as active participants in the planning, implementation, and evaluation of these programs. Another vital element in effective out-of-school programs is the strong involvement of parents and community members in all phases of the program. Generally, the activities provided in the programs include homework help, tutoring and other supplemental education services, creative arts and enrich ment, activities, youth leadership, recreation and athletics, drug and violence prevention strategies, and possibly some form of counseling or peer group discussions.

Note: Every one of the seven key elements of supportive learning environments presented in this chapter applies equally to all programs that take place outside of school time with modifications to the particular program and setting. Many excellent resources exist that provide program models, resources, and step-by-step implementation guidelines.

Web Resources
Afterschool.gov—A one-stop web site to federal resources that support children and youth during out-of-school hours http://www.afterschool.gov
21st Century Community Learning Center Programs The government site for 21st century community learning center-funded programs http://www.ed.gov/21stcclc
The Charles Stewart Mott Foundation Additional online resources relating to afterschool programs http://www.mott.org
Beyond the Bell: A Toolkit for Creating Effective After-School Programs http://www.ncrel.org/after/bellkit.htm
Harvard Family Research Project http://www.gse.harvard.edu/hfrp/projects/afterschool/evaldatabase.html

Element 4: Student-Centered Learning Practices

Picture Success: Teacher Practices
Teachers who effectively use student-centered learning practices: ■ See students as active inventors of meaning ■ Develop mechanisms for students to control their own learning ■ Involve students directly in exploring and discovering their world ■ Use innovative resources and materials that challenge students to use their prior knowledge and forge deeper understandings of concepts ■ Use multiple modalities that actively teach social skills such as cooperative learning, project-based learning, problem-based learning, role play, case study, jigsaws, and so on ■ Use community resources such as service learning and community service for learning ■ Involve all constituents in contributing to student learning (faculty, students, staff, family, community members) ■ Apply real life to learning beyond the classroom to create greater relevance and motivation for learning

Active versus Passive Learning

The old conceptions of the student as an empty vessel and the teacher as gatekeeper of knowledge are giving way to a new concept of student-centered learning. Modern thinking views students as active learners, taking responsibility for their own learning.

With increasing emphasis on education as a way to prepare students to enter the increasingly technological and complex workforce, skills in the classroom must directly relate to the skills in the world of work. Business leaders continually sound the call that to be successful in the marketplace, students today need to be able to solve complex problems, be technologically literate, get along with other people, and interact within a diverse team.

Being a passive learner subjected to mind-numbing drill-and-kill routines and rote learning techniques does not adequately prepare a student for today's world. Yet the teaching of social skills is often relegated to the realm of health and nonacademic arenas. These skills are integral to the learning process for all subject areas.

Programs and Practices

One of the most successful and well-used student-centered learning techniques is cooperative learning (Johnson & Johnson, 1999; Marzano, Pickering, & Pollock, 2001; Slavin, 1991), which has been shown to significantly affect learning, teach valuable social skills, and decrease dropping out.

Relating learning to life creates relevance and motivation for students to become engaged in the process of learning. Techniques that forge linkages between the school and community and provide opportunities for self-reflection, such as project-based learning, service learning, and community service (Duckenfield & Swanson, 1992; Shumer, 1994), and cross-age tutoring (Cardenas, Montecel, Supik, & Harris, 1992) have been proven effective at enhancing achievement, engaging students from diverse backgrounds, enhancing healthy behaviors, and school completion.

Performance feedback techniques have long been a part of management training, but only now are they considered vital to the teacher-student relationship. Practices such as providing students with specific, timely, corrective feedback as well as opportunities for students to create peer and self-assessments enhance student performance (Bangert-Downs, Kulik, Kulick & Morgan, 1991). The importance of traditional health-related skills such as personal goal setting and the resiliency skills of overcoming obstacles through problem solving and reinforcing effort further enhance student achievement in academic areas as well as provide valuable life skills (Bandura, 1977; Seligman, 1990).

Cooperative Learning

As the name implies, cooperative learning relies on students learning from each other in small groups. The learning becomes student-centered rather than teacher-centered. Teachers take the role of facilitator and guide. Students become more self-reliant and peer-focused, instilling a greater sense of responsibility for their own learning. They engage in higher-level problem solving because they become more-active learners in the discovery process.

Another advantage of cooperative learning is that it allows students of different races and abilities to work and learn together. This creates a more equitable classroom environment and enhances student interactions and social skills. Research has found that "students of low ability actually perform worse when they are placed in homogenous groups with students of low ability." (Marzano, Pickering & Pollock, 2001, p. 87) This would seem to suggest that heterogeneous ability groupings seem to hold the greatest benefit for the lowest achieving students.

Web Resource

Cooperative Learning Network

An association of colleagues at Sheridan Institute of Technology and Advanced Learning who model, share, support, and advocate for use of cooperative learning

http://www.sheridanc.on.ca/coop_learn/cooplrn.htm

Service Learning

Picture Success: Service Learning Projects

Students Dive into Politics

Students in Tri-Cities, Washington learn about history and the political system in school and become involved in politics outside of class. As part of a service-learning project in a social studies class, students have been speaking to homeowners about voting and registering people to vote.

Teaching Civics: A Call to Action

Hudson High School, in Hudson, Massachusetts increases student performance by restructuring to emphasize civic education classes, services-learning projects, and small learning communities. Students learn civic skills and have a voice in school governance. They participate in weekly cluster meetings and a community council, in which they can raise important issues.

—National Service Learning Partnerships Promising Practices

Service learning combines learning in the classroom with learning beyond the classroom through service to the school and community that meets identified needs. Students use the community as a learning environment—forging valuable connections to the community and to the world of work, and instilling a sense of social responsibility. Service learning reflects the beliefs that the most effective learning is active and that learning should be connected to experience. A key element of any service learning program is to provide opportunities for student reflection to deepen the learning experience in a meaningful way.

Many excellent resources exist to provide program ideas, strategies, research, and materials.

Web Resources

National Service Learning Clearinghouse
http://www.servicelearning.org

Learn and Serve America
http://www.learnandserve.org

National Service Learning Partnership
http://www.service-learningpartnership.org

Providing Recognition and Feedback

Picture Success: Guidelines for Providing Effective Feedback and Recognition

Teachers who provide effective feedback and recognition:

- Maintain high expectations of excellence for all students, regardless of gender, socioeconomic status, race, ability, or other personal characteristics
- Communicate clear and objective criteria for performance
- Hold students accountable for timely completion of work
- Hold students accountable for classroom behavior and participation
- Provide timely, specific feedback to students in private
- Tie recognition and rewards directly to student performance
- Provide private as well as public recognition
- Train students to provide effective peer feedback and reinforcement
- Involve students in peer and self-assessments and evaluation

Goal Setting Through Student Contracting

These two strategies are interrelated, providing feedback and recognition and teaching goal setting through student contracting. As discussed previously, feedback and recognition cannot be abstract or random; they must be tied to performance. When the relationship between effort and achievement is taught, students learn the skill of overcoming obstacles by reapplying problem-solving strategies and focusing on solutions rather than blame. Martin Seligman (1990) sees this as a major defining characteristic of learned optimism, a hallmark of resiliency.

Behavioral strategists have identified the skill of personal goal setting as a powerful motivator for changing behavior through what is termed the internal locus of control. Internal control provides intrinsic motivation as opposed to extrinsic motivation—or relying on the praise, recognition, or direction from others. When students have active opportunities to self-direct their learning by establishing personal goals through a formal contract, they are more likely to persist in the face of adversity and to achieve the desired goal. These same strategies are applied to learning the skills of resisting negative social influences in successful drug prevention programs (see Element 6).

Multicultural Competence

Refer to Chapter 2 for a more complete discussion on multicultural competence.

Element 5: Caring Relationships and Sense of Community

Young people don't care how much you know until they know how much you care.

Web Resource
The Wingspread Group A fine collection of articles on topics related to caring relationships and school community http://www.jhsph.edu/wingspread

It is one thing to call yourself an educator and an entirely different thing to have healthy relationships with children and young people. Relationships are the foundation on which learning is built. Forming mutually respectful relationships with young people involves establishing rapport, empathy, a common ground of understanding, and communication.

When a student truly experiences support from adults, they feel more connected to school. Their behavior becomes more cooperative and they exhibit fewer risk behaviors (Jenkins, 1996; Manlove, 1998). Their values reflect greater congruence with learning. As they become increasingly concerned with higher grades and test scores, they invest more time and energy in homework and they care more about what teachers think of them (Goodenow, 1993; Lee & Smith, 1999).

Adults too often rely on the power imbalance inherent in the adult/child relationship as a means of gaining control. This power play becomes a poor substitute for real respect and cooperation. As adults consciously include children and young people in the decision-making process and create more learner-centered environments, students are willing to obey and honor the requests of the adult through their adherence to rules and acceptable conduct (Baumeister & Leary, 1995; Brown & Evans, 2002). We as adults must earn that respect by communicating our genuine belief in young people, treating them in a respectful and equal manner, and providing active opportunities for shaping their learning environments. This is the mutual reciprocity that exists in respectful relationships.

Many young people are hungry for connections with adults outside of their families and immediate neighborhoods. How many of us can still remember a favorite teacher, principal, neighbor, or coach from our grade school years? A major distinguishing characteristic of resilient young people is their ability to extract support from seemingly nonsupportive environments. Despite a lack of adequate nurturance and guidance within the family or community, these resilient youth can locate individuals with whom they can form a caring and healthy bond. Indeed, the prosocial skills and motivation to form these relationships are part of the underlying characteristics of healthy behavior (Benson et al., 1999; Werner & Smith 1982, 1992; Rutter, 1987).

We cannot afford to become complacent as adults by relying on those resilient young people who reach out and connect with us. We must be willing and accessible to all youngsters, particularly the high-risk or hard to reach youth who might not have formed the prosocial skills necessary to support healthy relationships. These socially isolated young people are at particularly high risk for many problem behaviors, including substance use, suicide, gang affiliation, and other forms of violence (Hawkins, Smith, & Catalano, 2004; Jessor & Jessor, 1977). Making sure that every child is known by at least one adult (refer to Element 3) is a strong protective factor for these young people and for all youth.

Cultivating an attitude of respect and bearing witness to the potential in all human beings involves seeing all young people as resources, not entities to be acted on (Benard, 1997; Pittman, O'Brien, & Kimball, 1993). This is the essence of empowerment that underlies successful teaching.

High Expectations

Research has shown that academic achievement is highest in the context of expectations for academic success (referred to as *academic press*) combined with social supports for learners (Battistich et al., 1996; Lee & Smith, 1999). When only academic press is present, achievement suffers. A caring school is wonderful, but learning suffers without an emphasis on student achievement. One without the other diminishes achievement; both are necessary to help students perform well in school. Reported gains may be highest for the most at-risk students.

Evidence supports the role of teacher expectations as strongly influencing student achievement (Brophy, 1981; Eccles et al., 1993). A young person can discern the truth of an adult's feelings. They have the best hypocrisy detectors available, a kind of radar that allows them to know when an adult really likes them and believes in them, and when the adult is simply giving lip service. It is critical to examine our expectations as adults and move beyond mere lip service to action. We must be sure that we can truly convey our belief in children's ability to succeed, not just for some children but also for all children (Hilliard, 1991). Once again, the skill of multicultural competence is critical to this process (refer to Chapter 2).

The single most important asset you can give young people is your total unwavering belief in their ability to achieve. The picture of their success that you hold in your mind and heart is a felt entity between you and the young person in front of you. They feel it. They know it. They experience it as a spoken or unspoken expectation and respond with greater belief in themselves and their abilities. Actively teaching the relationship between effort and success enhances performance and creates a more optimistic attitude for students about school and learning (Connell & Wellborn, 1991; Marzano, Pickering, & Pollock, 2001; Seligman, 1990).

Creating a Learning Community

Mutual respect and reciprocal relationships extend to the adults within the learning community as well. Teachers report a higher sense of satisfaction when collaboration and a sense of community are high (Bryk & Driscoll, 1988; Lee et al., 1991). Teachers need ongoing opportunities to engage in collaborative inquiry and reflection. Working in teams to create a culture of learning and openness is a key to successful learning communities (Becker & Riel, 1999; Darling-Hammond, 1996; Sergiovanni, 1996; Smylie, 1994).

This means that the same qualities of listening, being nonjudgmental, and being willing to be challenged to grow and improve are inherent in the relationships between teachers and teachers, staff and administrators, school and parents, and school and community. The key to building strong relationships and partnerships in the improvement process starts with reflecting these same simple qualities of respect for all participants, regardless of formal rank or social stature.

Peer Relationships and Social Skills

Students' sense of connection to school is also influenced by relationships with peers. Students who report positive peer relationships also report a greater sense of attachment and engagement in school (Brown & Evans, 2002; Simons-Morton & Crump, 2002). Peer relations are clearly correlated with addressing bullying behavior in school through policies, interventions, and social skill building (Bodenhamer, Burger, and Prutzman, 1975; Kreidler, 1994). Respect, appreciation, and tolerance for diversity; conflict resolution; communication; and decision making are all skills that contribute to a supportive school community.

Element 6: Schoolwide Positive Discipline and Self-Management Practices

Social Skill Building and Behavior Management

The heart of any behavior management system in schools should start with a preventative approach through the active teaching of prosocial behaviors. Research on successful prevention programs has shown that teaching social skills to students results in greater levels of prosocial behavior (Dusenberry, 1996; Metis Associates, 1990; U. S. Depts. of Education and Justice, 2000). In Project ALERT, a validated middle school drug prevention program, students learn the skills of resisting social influences to use tobacco, marijuana, alcohol, and other drugs (Ellickson & Bell, 1990). Interactive learning methodologies such as role play, skill rehearsal, task groups, video trigger films, and contracting are employed. Another validated drug prevention program is Life Skills (Botvin et al., 1990) Students learn skills such as decision making, communication, goal setting, giving and receiving compliments, stress-reduction skills, and resisting negative influences to engage in risky behavior.

The Child Development Project (CDP) is a comprehensive, elementary school-based intervention program (Battistich et al., 1996). The central goal of CDP is to help schools become caring communities of learners by offering an environment of caring, supportive, and collaborative relationships to build students' sense of community in school and to promote school bonding. Other models use similar techniques that incorporate class meetings; learning activities for partners and small groups; and peer-led discussions on culturally relevant poetry, songs, literature, and current events to enhance students' social, ethical, and intellectual development (Holtz Frank, 2003).

(See also Elements 3 (page 42) and 4 (page 50) for other effective uses of these strategies.)

Web Resources

Drug Strategies

Provides the following resources:

- *Treating Teens: A Guide to Adolescent Drug Programs*
- *Revised Making the Grade: A Guide to School Drug Prevention Programs*
- *Safe Schools, Safe Students: A Guide to Violence Prevention Strategies*

  http://www.drugstrategies.org

Promising Practices Network

  http://www.promisingpractices.net/programlist.asp

Positive Classroom Management Techniques

Daily reinforcement of these prosocial skills should be modeled by adults and students across the curriculum. Techniques such as class meetings and discussions, student contracting, peer teaching, and interactive teaching methodologies serve to engage students in learning and self-managing their own behaviors (Battistich et al., 1996). Entrusting students of all ages with the capacity to learn these skills and manage many of the functions currently assigned to teachers is one of the joys of discovering how to design effective classroom and schoolwide management techniques with students rather than for them or to them (Freiberg, Connell, & Lorentz, 2001; Kohn, 1996).

Picture Success: Class Meetings

Donna Styles (2001) offers the following tips for successful class meetings:

- Use a formal process and hold meetings every week.
- Use a circle formation with members sitting in chairs.
- Model respectful behavior.
- Create a positive classroom environment.
- Do not dominate meetings.
- Have faith in the creative problem-solving process.
- Trust the ability of your students to lead meetings, participate in discussions, choose solutions, and make decisions that will affect the classroom.

Schoolwide Policies

Whenever I teach staff development sessions on school discipline and violence prevention, the number one risk factor in the school that educators always cite is the lack of a clearly communicated discipline policy. The number two risk factor they cite is the lack of consistent enforcement. Rather than the top-down hierarchical management style that is not part of shared leadership (refer to Element 2, page 40), discipline policies should be collaboratively designed with student and staff input. Positive behaviors need to be specifically taught to students, recognized, and reinforced. Students who are part of this type of collaboratively designed system report a greater sense of autonomy and self-regulate their behaviors, resulting in fewer referrals and discipline problems, higher achievement motivation, and a greater sense of school attachment and bonding (Brophy, 1981; Cameron & Pierce, 1994; Sugai, Horner, & Gresham, 2001).

Staff members also need to be sensitized and trained to engage in equal and proportionate enforcement across gender, socioeconomic, and racial groups (McFadden, Marsh, Price, & Hwang, 1992).

Recognition and Rewards for Positive Behavior

Many of the old school methods for rewarding children derive from a competitive model of rewarding some students at the expense of others. Many educators misunderstand the concept of rewards to mean the provision of external rewards. Applying external rewards to students can actually decrease desired behavior rather than increase it. The most effective method for reinforcing positive behaviors is to provide an equitable environment in which children and youth can feel safe, respected, and challenged (Kohn, 1996). In this type of safe and supportive learning environment, students find their own intrinsic motivation for learning and do not need to be externally rewarded. However, when a school is shifting from a reliance on more punitive methods to one that emphasizes positive self-managed behaviors, or students have had no prior exposure to this type of environment, extrinsic rewards can be helpful. Training should be provided to all staff in the building, including bus drivers, teachers' aides, lunch and playground monitors, and others on effective methods for personalizing positive feedback, rewards, and recognition. An environment that creates individualized goals and recognizes goal attainment for all students, not just the highest achievers, provides incentives and motivation for students to achieve academically as well as socially and behaviorally (Seligman, 1990; Sugai, Horner, & Gresham, 2001; Sugai, Sprague, Horner, & Walker, 2001). Refer to Element 4 for more information.

Web Resource
Center for Effective Collaboration and Practice Excellent resources for helping communities create schools that promote emotional well-being http://cecp.air.org/guide/actionguide/Resources.htm

Element 7: Active Staff, Student, Family, and Community Involvement

(Refer to Chapter 2 for more information on building school-community teams.)

Community Involvement

Positively affecting the lives of young people involves a willingness to work across systems, in a collaborative endeavor aimed at strengthening the fabric of the whole community, not just selective parts. It requires a change in thinking and in practice. Creating this community web of connection is one of the most significant challenges faced today in the field of school improvement.

To be an effective change agent within our schools and communities means remaining accountable to the young people and families that we serve. Accountability involves starting with a constituent base or planning team that is culturally representative of the full range of diversity for the whole community (taking into account issues of race, ethnicity, socioeconomic status, gender, religion, physical and mental ability, sexual orientation, and age). The primary power brokers within the school (usually the administrators such as the superintendent, assistant superintendents, principals, etc.) must be responsive to the community and be willing to share power, to adapt the decision-making process to reflect accurately the community's input. This includes allowing significant youth voice, as well as full participation from family and community in creating the structures, programs, policies, and processes that affect the lives and achievement of young people. (Comer, Haynes, Joyner, & Ben-Avie, 1996; Pittman, 1991; Schargel & Smink, 2001).

The reluctance of some administrators (and indeed adults in general) to share power is understandable. There is a very real discomfort and readjustment that this may cause. The trade-off comes from viewing the results of successful school and community collaborations. Among the results reported from these partnerships are improved school attendance, reading and math scores, reduction in suspensions (Dryfoos, 1998), and significant decrease in dropout rates, particularly with high-risk youth (Cardenas et al., 1992).

Family Involvement

Research provides compelling evidence that family involvement in children's education promotes student achievement and decreases the likelihood that students will drop out (Henderson & Berla, 1995). Parents can be involved in school in a variety of ways, including developing school policy, attending school functions, communicating with their child's teacher, assisting with homework, attending parent education classes, attending adult education classes, acting as a parent peer leader or educator, and becoming involved in specific intervention programs designed for families (Balli, 1998; Epstein, 1995; Hawkins et al., 1987; Perkins & Milgram, 1996). The key to parental involvement, as with any other constituency, is to elicit parent participation from the inception so parents can design or tailor existing programs to their needs.

Youth Involvement

It is no longer feasible in the 21st century to expect success from innovations or strategies that maintain the often-unspoken belief that children should be seen and not heard. Young people are exposed to far too many social influences at younger and younger ages to accept a passive role in their world. They have capabilities, emerging competencies, and a unique perspective that adds the vital element of youth flavor to any endeavor attempting to address the issues of contemporary youth. The field of youth development encourages and advocates youth engagement at all levels in developing programs, from inception to culmination (Benard, 1990; Carnegie Council on Adolescent Development, 1989; Pittman & Wright, 1991). Youth involvement can take many forms in the community, including community service, volunteering service, learning (Duckenfeld & Swanson, 1992; Shumer, 1994), cross-age tutoring—as in the successful Coca Cola Valued Youth Program (Cardenas et al., 1992), advocacy, planning, media relations, and many other youth-generated ideas.

Successful teaching and learning within the schools must also include youth participation and involvement. Creating a sense of community means establishing mechanisms with students for classroom and schoolwide student involvement (Battistich et al., 1996). Proactive strategies of student self-management, self-discipline, and choice-centered and learner-centered approaches (discussed earlier in this chapter) all reflect active student participation.

This youth participation can be extremely challenging for many adults and professionals who have erroneously been taught that maintaining strict control at all times is a necessary aspect of teaching. In fact, research has shown that controlling teachers do not increase student achievement, in fact. Educators who build inclusive relationships that engage students and allow autonomous decision making are more likely to see gains in academic achievement (Connell & Wellborn, 1991; Deci & Ryan, 1985). This requires conscious effort to examine our own professional practice, behaviors and motivations, and an unrelenting willingness to change and grow as a human being.

Staff Involvement

Research has found that teachers who are actively engaged in school decision making and who enjoy collegial relationships within the school in turn allow greater student involvement and leadership in the classroom (Becker & Riel, 1999; Smylie, 1994). Staff involvement, just as with the involvement of other stakeholders, serves to enhance a sense of being a part of a learning community and increases motivation, sense of self-efficacy, and satisfaction (Darling-Hammond, 1996; Sergiovanni, 1996). At a time when we are concerned with teacher retention, shouldn't we be paying more attention to the needs and active involvement of staff within our community of learners?

Web Resources
Search Institute http://www.search-institute.org
40 Developmental Assets framework: Forum for Youth Investment Youth development http://www.forumforyouthinvestment.org/organization.htm
Harvard Family Research Project:: Family-school partnerships http://www.gse.harvard.edu/hfrp/projects/family.html
WestEd: School-community partnerships http://www.wested.org/online_pubs/po-02-04.pdf

Indicators of Success

Figures 3.2 through 3.8 (page 65–77) show the seven key elements, with a checklist of indicators of success for each and an extensive list of researchers in the various areas.

Figure 3.1. Seven Key Elements of Supportive Learning Environments: The Research Base

Element 1:	Safety of the Physical Plant
Element 2:	Shared Leadership Practices
Element 3:	Structured Personalized Learning Communities
Element 4:	Student Centered Learning Practices
Element 5:	Caring Relationships and Sense of Community
Element 6:	Schoolwide Positive Discipline and Self-Management Practices
Element 7:	Active Student, Staff, Family, and Community Involvement

Figure 3.2. Element 1: Safety of the Physical Plant

1 = Not evident 2 = Somewhat or occassionally evident 3 = Consistently evident 4 = Consistently evident and provides an excellent exemplar	Rubric			
Indicators of Success	**1**	**2**	**3**	**4**
▪ Clean walls inside and out with no graffiti				
▪ Clean hallways and classrooms with no garbage or debris				
▪ Well lit hallways, bathrooms, and classrooms				
▪ Wide hallways and stairs				
▪ Windows and natural light				
▪ Offices are located near main entrance				
▪ Policies are enforced regarding visitor sign in at front entrance				
▪ Bathrooms are located in main traffic area, not in isolated locations				
▪ Classrooms are clustered by grade level				
▪ School can safely accommodate all students, is not overcrowded				
▪ Security is monitored through surveillance technology, cameras, alarms, two-way radios and/or "human" detectors				
▪ Isolated areas, if they exist, are closely monitored				
▪ Clean air that meets standard Federal (OSHA) requirements				
▪ Safety plan well developed and clearly communicated				
▪ Parents, families, community members, and representatives are involved in the development of the safety plan				
▪ Plan is periodically practiced and refined				
▪ Appropriate linkages with law enforcement and other agencies and services are maintained on a regular basis.				
Fein, R. A., Vossekuil, B., Pollack, W. S., Borum, R., Modzeleski, W., & Reddy, M., 2002; Jalloh, M. & Fuchs Nadeau, D. 2000; Safe Schools, Safe Students, 1998; Schneider, Walker, & Sprague, 2000; U.S. Department of Education & Justice, 2000				

Figure 3.3. Element 2: Shared Leadership Practices

Indicators of Success	Rubric			
	1	2	3	4
Provides Shared Leadership				
■ Acts as a positive change agent for school improvement.				
■ Communicates clear vision and shared beliefs.				
■ Encourages responsibility for leadership at all levels of the organization.				
■ Operates from strong and consistent ethical core values.				
■ Displays respect for all people and values diversity.				
■ Provides mechanisms for consistent feedback and positive reinforcement across the organization.				
■ Provides clear and orderly infrastructure with a focus on teaching and learning.				
■ Willing to be innovative and challenge conventional thinking.				
■ Understands the systemic nature and order of interventions to ensure lasting growth and change.				
■ Builds in accountability mechanisms at all levels.				
Creates a professional learning community				
■ Models continuous learning and teaching.				
■ Promotes and models use of reflection and critical analysis.				
■ Conveys a sense of a community of learners.				
■ Actively develops leadership of learners including students and parents.				
■ Engages in regular quality learning interactions with staff, students, parents, and community members.				
■ Provides staff and students with current resources.				
■ Provides all staff with professional development opportunities.				
■ Actively provides outreach to and shares resources with parents and community.				
■ Celebrates accomplishments and acknowledges need for improvement.				
Creates clear communication between and among all stakeholders				
■ Communicates regularly with staff and students.				
■ Fosters collaborative and respectful relationships with all stakeholders. Provides public dissemination of information to parents and community.				
■ School employs a variety of communication methods including media outlets, letters, website.				
■ Key results of school improvement are reported to families and community.				
■ Key results are disaggregated by student groupings for low income, minority, and students with disability, etc.				
Coordination of existing school improvement efforts				
■ School teams are developed including a broad representation of school staff, student, parent, and community members.				
■ School improvement efforts are developed in coordination with existing efforts rather than as isolated strategies.				
■ Data is used to inform efforts and provide continuous improvement.				
■ Goals are jointly established, clearly communicated, and strategically implemented.				
Bennis, 1997; Covey, 1989; Elmore, 2000; Hilliard, 1991; Senge, 1990; Sergiovanni, 1994; Tichy, 2002; Waters, Marzano, & McNulty, 2003				

Figure 3.4. Element 3: Structured Personalized Learning Communities

Indicators of Success: Learning Communities	Rubric			
	1	2	3	4
Small Schools				
■ Defined as 600–900 students				
■ Teachers and administrators report more positive attitudes and collaboration				
■ Students report a greater sense of belonging				
■ Students have a perception of more support and caring				
■ Achievement gains				
■ Greatest gains may be for poor and minority students				
■ Enhanced school attendance				
■ Increased school completion rates				
■ Increased student participation in extracurricular activities				
Allen, L., & Steinberg, A. 2004; Cotton, 1998; Lee & Smith, 1997; Seidman, et al, 1996; Wasley, 2000				
Schools within Schools				
■ School divided into teams or "houses"				
■ Small, stable student groups				
Oakes & Guiton, 1995				
Small Class Size				
■ Defined as 15–20 students per class				
■ Positive gains on achievement				
■ Greatest gains may be for poor and minority students				
■ More individualized attention				
■ Students report better relationships with their peers and their teacher				
U.S. Department of Education, 1999				
Looping				
■ Teachers stay with same class for two or more grade levels				
■ Students experience more successful transitions				
■ Students improve in social skills				
■ Better relationship between peers, students and teachers, and teachers and parents				
■ Parents are also more likely to participate within the school				
■ Teachers benefit from time saved in initial assessment & reintroduction to student and family				
Denault, 1999; National Association of Secondary School Principals, 2004				

Indicators of Success: Learning Communities	Rubric			
	1	2	3	4
Advisory Programs				
■ Every student is known by at least one adult				
■ Advisors have daily interactions with students				
■ Effective practices are utilized in the design and implementation of an advisory program				
■ Staff receives adequate training in the role of advisor				
■ Staff are trained in making appropriate referrals				
■ Advisory programs are made available to all students				
Ayres, L., 1994; Carnegie Corp., 1989; Education Alliance, 2003; Holtz Frank, 1996; Stevenson, C. 1992; National Middle School Association, 1996				
Mentoring Programs				
■ Establish a mentoring relationship with prosocial adults and older students				
■ Effective practices are utilized in the design and implementation of mentoring program				
■ Mentors and program supervisors receive adequate training				
■ Increased scholastic competence				
■ Program may have greatest impact on substance abuse reductions for minority boys				
LoSciuto, Rajala, Townsend, & Taylor, 1996; Tierney, Grossman, Resch, 1995				
Transition Programs				
■ Especially important entering and leaving middle schoolatio				
■ Provide students and parents with informn about new school				
■ Provide students with social support				
■ Involve parents in program				
■ Bring together staff from the two schools to learn about one another's programs				
■ May be combined with mentoring program				
■ Increases student achievement and reduces dropouts				
Adelman & Taylor, 2002; Eccles, Lord & Midgley, 1991; Mac Iver, 1990; Schumacher, 1998				
After School and Extended Day Programs				
■ Connect to the school day				
■ Provide homework help, tutoring and other supplemental education services				
■ Have strong youth development focus				
■ Provide enrichment activities				
■ Provide drug and violence prevention strategies				
■ Engage family, school, and community as active partners				
Schinke, 1999; U.S. Dept. of Ed. (2003)				

Indicators of Success: Learning Communities	Rubric			
	1	2	3	4
Continuum of Supports				
■ Wide range of services are available for prevention, early intervention, and intensive intervention				
■ Strong linkages with community referral sources				
■ Parents are involved in service delivery				
■ Staff are trained in Federal and State confidentiality and reporting requirements				
■ Staff are trained in recognizing behavioral signs and symptoms of students in need of counseling and how to make referrals				
■ Counseling is used appropriately to support behavioral interventions				
■ Community resources are effectively utilized				
■ Alternative placement is available and appropriately used				
Adelman & Taylor, 2002; Dryfoos, 1994 ; Holtz Frank, 1996				

Figure 3.5. Element 4: Student Centered Learning Practices

Indicators of Success: Student Centered Learning	Rubric			
	1	2	3	4
Student centered instruction and assessment practices are employed.				
■ Teachers are trained in student centered learning techniques.				
■ Students are encouraged to control their own learning through contracting around setting goals, subgoals and corresponding grades.				
■ Students are given opportunities for self assessment and student-led feedback.				
■ Teachers encourage students to personalize learning and instructional goals.				
■ Teachers engage in contracting with students around learning goals.				
Deci & Ryan, 1985; Marzano, Pickering, & Pollock, 2001				
Cooperative learning is effectively utilized.				
■ Staff is trained in techniques of effective use of cooperative learning strategies.				
■ Heterogeneous ability groupings are applied more often than homogenous grouping.				
■ Students learn social skills along with content.				
■ Enhances learning.				
■ Performance enhancement may be highest for the lowest performing students.				
■ Promotes equity in the classroom.				
Johnson & Johnson, 1999; Slavin, 1991				
Community Service and Service Learning Programs				
Staff is trained in techniques of effective use of these learning strategies.				
Student reflection and self assessment are built into program.				
Students exhibit skills in personal and social development.				
Students display civic responsibility.				
Strengthens school-youth-community relationships.				
Students develop self-reflection practices.				
Service experience connects learning to life for students.				
Student participation significantly reduced dropout rate.				
Cardenas, Montecel, Supik & Harris, 1992; Duckenfeld & Swanson, 1992; Holtz Frank, 2003; Schargel & Smink, 2001; Shumer, 1994				

Indicators of Success: Student Centered Learning	Rubric			
	1	2	3	4
Students receive individualized performance feedback.				
■ Teachers are trained in providing effective feedback.				
■ Teachers are trained in effective assessment practices.				
■ Teachers are trained in giving effective positive reinforcement and personal recognition to students.				
■ Public displays of student work.				
■ Families are aware of students' achievements.				
■ Community is aware of students' achievements.				
Bangert-Downs, Kulick, Kulick, & Morgan, 1991; Brophy, 1981; Marzano, Pickering, Pollock, 2001; Meier, 1995; Seligman, 1990				
Multicultural Competence				
■ Staff and students receive training in multicultural competence.				
■ Staff and students demonstrate ability to relate to diverse populations.				
■ Staff and students actively monitor attitudes and actions to avoid stereotyping or biased behavior.				
■ Staff and students display active awareness of how one's attitudes affect one's behavior toward others.				
■ Staff exhibit high expectations for all students and families.				
■ Staff exhibit equitable interactions with all students and families.				
■ Students learn how to interact fairly and equitably with others of different race, ethnicity, gender.				
Chisom & Washington, 1977; Delpit, 1995; Nieto, 1992; Noguera, 2003; North Central Regional Educational Laboratory, 2004; Payne, 1996; Perry, Steele, & Hilliard, 2003; Rothstein, 2004; Tatum, 1991				

Figure 3.6. Element 5: Caring Relationships and Sense of Community

Indicators of Success: Relationships and Community	Rubric			
	1	2	3	4
Positive, high expectations for all students				
■ Teacher expectations influence students' achievement.				
■ School encourages high expectations for all students.				
■ Constant emphasis on academic achievement (academic press) combined with strong emphasis on student support.				
■ Academic achievement is high or increasing.				
■ Students report a strong sense of support from school.				
■ When students perceive school as community, achievement gains may be greatest for the most at-risk students.				
Battistich, Schaps, Watson, Solomon, 1996; Brophy, 1981; Eccles, et al. 1993; Lee & Smith, 1999; Marzano, R. J., Pickering, D. J., Pollock, J. E., 2001				
Every student has a trusting relationship with at least one adult				
■ At least one adult is personally assigned to every student.				
■ Student advisory teams.				
■ Team teaching.				
■ Looping is used, keeping student with same teacher multiple years.				
■ Adult knows student's academic progress, daily attendance, family situation.				
Benson, P. L., Scales, P. C., Leffert, N., & Roehlkpartain, E. C., 1999; Carnegie Council on Adolescent Development, 1989; Gottfredson, 2001				
Students experience support from adults				
■ Students report that teachers and adults care about them.				
■ Students report that teachers provide extra help and guidance when needed.				
■ Students report that teachers listen to them.				
■ Students report that teachers praise them.				
■ Students report having opportunities to make decisions.				
■ Students report clear sense of structure.				
■ Students display higher academic achievement.				
Battistich & Horn, 1997; Connell & Wellborn, 1991; Deci & Ryan, 1985; Goodenow, 1993; Klem & Connell, 2004; Lee & Smith, 1999; Freiberg, 1988; Ryan & Patrick, 2001; Voelkl, 1995				
Teachers' sense of community				
■ Teachers report a high degree of satisfaction.				
■ Teacher collaboration is high.				
■ Teachers promote a stronger sense of community to students.				
Bryk & Driscoll, 1988; Hilliard, 1991; Lee, Dedrick, & Smith, 1991; Little & McLauglhin, 1993				

Indicators of Success: Relationships and Community	Rubric			
	1	2	3	4
Strong sense of school as community & positive school climate.				
■ School engagement is high or increasing.				
■ Students actively participate in school events.				
■ Academic motivation is high.				
■ Students abide by school rules, norms and values.				
■ Students and adults have good relationships.				
■ When students perceive school as community achievement gains may be greatest for the most at-risk students.				
Battistich, et al 1995; Battistich & Horn, 1997; Noddings, 1992; Schaps, Battistich, & Solomon, 1997				
Students feel a sense of bonding and belonging.				
■ Students accept the goals of school.				
■ Students display fewer risk behaviors.				
■ Students report feeling a part of school.				
■ Students report commitment and attachment to school.				
■ Students care about what teachers think of them.				
Baumeister & Leary, 1995; Brown & Evans, 2002; Finn, 1993; Hawkins et al. 2004; Hirschi, 1969; Voelkl, 1996; Werner & Smith, 1992				
Students are academically engaged in school.				
■ Students display more positive attitudes towards school.				
■ Students spend time on academic learning in and out of school.				
■ Students display greater tendency to stay on task and exert effort.				
■ Students see academics as useful in the future.				
■ Students exhibit fewer risk behaviors.				
Finn, 1993; Goodenow, 1993; Jenkins,1996; Jessor et al. 1977; Lee & Smith, 1999; Manlove, 1998; Resnick, et al. 1997				
Students display a more optimistic attitude toward school.				
■ Students reengage and apply effort in the face of challenge.				
■ Students exert problem-solving strategies when confronted with challenges.				
Connell & Wellborn, 1991, 1994; Marzano, Pickering, Pollock, 2001; Seligman, 1990; Skinner et al. 1990				

Indicators of Success: Relationships and Community	Rubric			
	1	2	3	4
Students have positive peer relations.				
■ Students report having friends at school.				
■ Students report having students they like on their classes.				
■ Students report few feelings of loneliness and alienation from school.				
Brown & Evans, 2002; Simons-Morton & Crump, 2002				
Safe environment is free from bullying and teasing.				
■ Policies address prevention and intervention of bullying and teasing behavior.				
■ Staff and students actively monitor and address behavior to ensure a bullying-free environment.				
■ Conflict resolution and diversity skills are taught and practiced by all.				
■ Policies and practices support open communication and breaking the code of silence.				
Bodenhamer, Burger, Prutzman, 1975; Fein, Vossekuil, Pollack, Borum, Modzeleski, Reddy, 2002; Jalloh, Fuchs Nadeau, 2000; Kreidler, 1994; Olweus, 1993				
Social and emotional needs are valued along with academic skills.				
■ Social and emotional skills are taught to students and adults.				
■ Em phasis is placed on emotional intelligence.				
■ Active listening is taught and valued.				
Battistich, Schaps, Watson, & Solomon, 1996; Elias et al. 1994; Goleman, 1995; Resnick, et al. 1997				
Multicultural Competence is taught and practiced.				
■ See 4. Student Centered Learning Practices				

Figure 3.7. Element 6: Schoolwide Positive Discipline and Self-Management Practices

Indicators of Success: Schoolwide Positive Discipline and Self Management	Rubric			
	1	2	3	4
Positive decision making, self management, and social skills are taught.				
■ Curriculum is taught using evidence based practices.				
■ Skills are taught and reinforced including anger management, effective communication techniques, conflict resolution, goal setting, self management, resistance skills, stress reduction.				
■ Service learning strategies are employed.				
Battistich, Schaps, Watson, & Solomon, 1996; Botvin et al. 1983, 1990; Catalano, Berglund, Ryan, Lonczak, & Hawkins, 2002; Dusenberry, 1996; Ellickson & Bell, 1990; Holtz Frank, 2003; Kohn, 1996; Johnson & Johnson, 1996; Metis Assoc., 1990; Safe Schools, Safe Students,1998; U.S. Department of Education & Justice, 2000				
Daily reinforcement of decision making, self management, and social skills.				
■ Skill practice is incorporated into daily activities.				
■ Skills and concepts are infused across curriculum.				
■ Self management practices are actively employed in the school and classroom.				
Positive classroom management.				
■ Positive behaviors are taught and reinforced.				
■ Students and teachers report a positive student-teacher relationships.				
■ Increase in instructional time.				
■ Improved classroom climate reported by students and teachers.				
■ More interactive teaching strategies are employed.				
■ Students have input into classroom rules.				
■ Students are engaged as classroom managers.				
Freiberg, Connell, & Lorentz, 2001; Sugai, et al. 2001a				
Consistent and fair enforcement of rules.				
■ Input is actively solicited and incorporated into schoolwide rule making from all constituent groups including students, parents, and faculty.				
■ Positive behavior is taught and reinforced.				
■ Positive behaviors are consistently recognized and rewarded.				
■ Opportunities are provided to students to correct their mistakes.				
■ Pro-social behavior is increased.				
■ Students report a greater sense of school bonding.				
■ Students report clear sense of expectations.				
Gottfredson, 2001; Pyper, Freiberg, Ginsburg, & Spuck, 1987; Resnick, Bearman, Blum, 1997; Sugai, et al. 2001a, 2001b				

Indicators of Success: Schoolwide Positive Discipline and Self Management	Rubric			
	1	2	3	4
Equitable discipline policy.				
■ Equal, proportionate enforcement across gender, socioeconomic, and racial groups.				
■ All students experience positive statements from staff made about them in their presence (preferably at a ratio of three positives for every negative).				
■ Monitoring suspensions, expulsions, and alternative placements to avoid disproportionate representation of minorities in suspensions, expulsions, and discipline referrals.				
McFadden, Marsh, Price, & Hwang, 1992; Skiba & Reece, 1997				
Personalized recognition, rewards, and praise in a cooperative, noncompetitive environment.				
■ Staff provides at least three positive statements for each negative statement made to students.				
■ Input is actively solicited and incorporated into schoolwide recognition and reward for positive student and adult behavior from all constituent groups including students, parents, and faculty.				
■ Staff is trained in providing appropriate choices and autonomy to students.				
■ Staff is trained in providing effective recognition and rewards for positive student behavior.				
■ Public displays of student work for all students.				
■ Public display and recognition for achievement in academics, attendance, effort for all students.				
■ Families are aware of students' achievements.				
■ Community is aware of students' achievements.				
Brophy, J., 1981; Cameron, J., & Pierce, W. D., 1994; Marzano, R. J., Pickering, D. J., Pollock, J. E., 2001; Seligman, 1990; Sugai et al. 2001				

Figure 3.8. Element 7: Active Staff, Student, Family, and Community

Involvement Indicators of Success: Active Staff, Student, Family, and Community Involvement	Rubric			
	1	2	3	4
Staff Involvement				
A learning community is developed and encouraged.				
■ Teachers are actively involved in learning and teaching at all levels.				
■ Teachers are provided with opportunities to engage in collaborative inquiry and reflection.				
■ Staff are provided with ongoing staff development to ensure continued learning and skill development.				
Becker & Riel, 1999; Darling-Hammond, 1996; Sergiovanni, 1996; Smylie, 1994				
Staff are given opportunities to provide input into school decisions.				
■ Teachers actively participate in school decision-making teams.				
■ Teachers who are actively engaged as decision makers in turn allow greater student involvement and leadership in the classroom.				
■ Mechanisms exist for open communication and feedback from all levels of staff.				
Active Student Involvement				
Opportunities for meaningful student engagement and participation.				
■ Mechanisms exist schoolwide for eliciting student voice in school policies.				
■ Students are involved in classroom management.				
■ Students have input into the development of schoolwide rules.				
■ Students are given appropriate choice in content areas; what and how content is taught.				
■ Students report a greater sense of safety.				
■ Academic achievement gains.				
■ Students report greater satisfaction and autonomy.				
Benard, 1990; Brown & Evans, 2002; Carnegie Council on Adolescent Development, 1989; Connell & Wellborn, 1991; Deci & Ryan, 1985; Hawkins, Smith & Catalano, 2004; Pittman & Wright, 1991; Resnick et al. 1997				
Student participation in extracurricular activities.				
■ Students attend school functions.				
■ Better attendance in school.				
■ Higher school completion rates.				
■ Higher aspirations.				
Brown & Evans, 2002; Jenkins, 1996; Nettles, Mucherah, & Jones, 2000				

Involvement Indicators of Success: Active Staff, Student, Family, and Community Involvement	Rubric 1	2	3	4
Students receive support for school from family.				
■ Family is involved in school.				
■ Family supports educational aspirations for student.				
■ Student shares educational values of parents.				
■ Students perceive linkage between family and school as a learning community.				
Comer, 1996; Epstein, 1995; Lewis, Schaps, & Watson, 1995; Viadero, 1994				
Parent and Family Involvement				
School actively seeks parental involvement K-12 in child's education.				
■ School continues to seek parental involvement in child's education K-12				
■ School seeks partnerships with parents to develop transition, afterschool programming, etc.				
■ Students have higher achievement and less likelihood of dropping out when parents are actively involved.				
Benson, Leffert, Scales, & Blyth, 1999; Comer, 1986; Epstein, 1995; Henderson & Berla, 1995				
Parents are actively involved in developing school policy.				
■ Parents are involved in school committees on safety, rules, codes of conduct, and school goals.				
Parents are actively invited to attend presentations and information sessions.				
■ Parents are invited to presentations to gain information about the school.				
■ Parents are encouraged and welcomed to visit school frequently.				
■ Parents are encouraged to attend school events.				
Schools are responsive to families needs through scheduling.				
■ Schools consult families to determine the most convenient time to schedule events, meetings, etc.				
■ Schools offer a choice of scheduling options to families.				
Positive respectful relationship between school and families.				
■ School exhibits multicultural competence in its ability to reach out to diverse sectors of the community.				
School staff is trained in effective communication techniques with parents.				
■ Staff receives ongoing training in how to communicate effectively with parents.				
■ Staff receives training in multicultural competence to enhance ability to relate to diverse populations.				
School emphasizes frequent, positive communication with parents.				
■ Staff are trained to emphasize student strengths in communicating with parents.				
■ School has clear policies on effective communication with parents.				
■ School develops two way communication methods for parents to contact the school through phone, notes, email, and direct contact.				

Involvement Indicators of Success: Active Staff, Student, Family, and Community Involvement	Rubric			
	1	2	3	4
Parents are aware of their child's progress in school.				
■ School actively informs parents of child's progress.				
■ School has a variety of communication methods for reaching parents including letters, phone, email, and media outlets.				
Parents are actively involved in developing and implementing parent involvement strategies.				
■ School includes parents as partners in developing strategies for parents.				
■ Parents are instrumental in determining how to effectively uncover and meet parent needs.				
■ Parents are utilized as resources in the delivery of parent services.				
Parents are instructed about the most effective methods for involvement in homework.				
■ Mechanisms exist for receiving information on homework assignments such as homework hotlines, assignment books, etc.				
■ Parents receive information about effective practices in assisting their children with homework.				
Balli, 1998; Perkins & Milgram, 1996				
Community Involvement				
Schoolwide teams are trained in data analysis.				
■ School provides basic training in gathering, interpreting, and summarizing data and identifying behavioral trends.				
■ Training is provided prior to goal setting and strategy implementation.				
Bernhardt, 1998; Wellman & Lipton, 2004				
School welcomes community involvement through active outreach.				
■ School extends direct invitations to community organizations, government organizations, businesses, faith-based organizations and nonprofit agencies to participate in school activities (such as Meet the Parents Night, Afterschool Programs, etc.).				
■ School actively recruits diverse groups through direct outreach.				
Benson, Leffert, Scales, & Blyth, 1999; Cardenas, Montecel, Supik,. & Harris, 1992; Comer, 1996; Dryfoos, 1994; Pittman, 1991; Safe Schools, Safe Students, 1998; Sanders, 2001; Wehlage, Rutter, Smith, Lesko, & Fernandez, 1989				
Community is seen as a resource.				
■ Community beliefs, values and culture are viewed as an asset.				
■ Community is utilized for social, cultural, and vocational resources.				
■ Schools respect the unique contribution from community and do not impose school structure on collaborative school/community programs.				
■ Formal and informal leadership (nonpositional power) structures are respected.				

Involvement Indicators of Success: Active Staff, Student, Family, and Community Involvement	Rubric			
	1	2	3	4
School collaborates with community resources to expand student and family supports.				
■ School develops a collaborative relationship of referrals to medical, mental health, area colleges, local businesses, and other agencies and organizations in the community including school-based health centers, youth service centers, community schools, and family resource centers.				
■ School collaborates with community in work related resource development.				
Positive respectful relationship between school and families.				
■ School exhibits multicultural competence in its ability to reach out to diverse sectors of the community.				
Community is actively involved in developing and implementing community involvement strategies.				
■ School includes community as partners in developing strategies to meet the needs of students and their families.				
■ Community is instrumental in determining how to effectively uncover and meet school/community needs.				
■ Community members and organizations are utilized as resources in the delivery of services such as internships, service learning, etc.				
School and community are accountable to each other.				
■ Schools and community members and agencies use collaborative rather than bureaucratic structures.				
■ Ongoing assessment and evaluations procedures are implemented.				
■ Results of evaluations and information is openly communicated reciprocally between school and community.				
School actively partners with community in developing programs.				
■ School seeks partnerships with the community to develop afterschool programming, community mobilization efforts, etc.				
■ Schools engage in shared leadership and decision making with community partners.				
Community is actively involved in developing school policy.				
■ Community members are involved in school committees on safety, rules, codes of conduct, and school goals.				
Community members are actively invited to attend presentations and information sessions.				
■ Community members are invited to presentations to gain information about the school.				
■ Community members are encouraged to attend school events.				
■ School has a variety of communication methods for reaching out to the community including letters, phone, email, and media outlets.				

References

Adelman, H. S., & Taylor, L. (2002). Building comprehensive, multifaceted and integrated approaches to address barriers to student learning. *Childhood Education, 78,* 261–268.

Allen, L., & Steinberg, A. (2004). *Big buildings, small schools: Using a small schools strategy for high school reform.* Providence, RI: Jobs for the Future: Prepared for Carnegie Corporation of New York and the Northeast and Islands Regional Educational Laboratory at Brown University.

Ayres, L. (1994, January). Middle school advisory programs: Findings from the field. *Middle School Journal,* 8–14.

Balli, S. J. (1998). When mom and dad help: Student reflections on parent involvement with homework. *Journal of Research and Development in Education, 31*(3), 142–148.

Bandura, A. (1977). Self-efficacy: Toward a unifying theory of behavioral change. *Psychological Review, 84,* 191–215.

Bandura, A. (1997). *Social learning theory.* Englewood Cliffs, NJ: Prentice Hall.

Bangert-Downs, R. I., Kulik, C. C., Kulick, J. A., & Morgan, M. (1991). The instructional effects of feedback in test-like events. *Review of Educational Research, 61*(2), 213–238.

Battistich, V., & Horn, A. (1997). The relationship between students' sense of their school as a community and their involvement in problem behavior. *American Journal of Public Health, 87*(12),1997–2001.

Battistich, V., Schaps, E., Watson, M., & Solomon, D. (1996). Prevention effects of the Child Development Project: Early findings from an ongoing multi-site demonstration trial. *Journal of Adolescent Research, 11*(1), 12–35.

Battistich, V., Solomon, D., Kim, D., Watson, M., & Schaps, E. (1995). Schools as communities, poverty levels of student populations, and students' attitudes, motives, and performance: A multilevel analysis. *American Educational Research Journal, 32,* 627–658.

Baumeister, R., & Leary, M. (1995). The need to belong: Desire for interpersonal attachments as a fundamental human motivation. *Psychological Bulletin, 117,* 497–529.

Becker, B. J., & Riel, M. M. (1999). *Teacher professionalism, school work culture and the emergence of constructivist-compatible pedagogies.* Presented at annual meeting of American Educational Research Association, Montreal.

Benard, B. (1990). *Youth service: From youth as problems to youth as resources.* Portland, OR: Northwest Regional Educational Laboratory.

Benard, B. (1997). *Turning it around for all youth; from risk to resilience.* ERIC/CUE Digest no. 126. New York: Eric Clearinghouse on Urban Education.

Bennis, W., & Goldsmith, J. (1997). *Learning to lead: A workbook on becoming a leader.* Cambridge, MA: Perseus.

Benson, P. L., Scales, P. C., Leffert, N., & Roehlkepartain, E. C. (1999). *A fragile foundation: The state of developmental assets among American youth.* Minneapolis: Search Institute.

Bernhardt, V. (1998). *Data analysis for comprehensive schoolwide improvement.* Larchmont, NY: Eye on Education.

Bodenhamer, G., Burger, M., & Prutzman, P. (1975). *Children's Creative Response to Conflict program.* New York: Quaker Project on Community Conflict.

Botvin, G. J. (1983). Prevention of adolescent substance abuse through the development of personal and social competence. *National Institute on Drug Abuse: Research Monograph Series, 47,* 115–140.

Botvin, G. J., Baker, E., Dusenbury, L., Tortu, S., & Botvin, E. M. (1990). Preventing adolescent drug abuse through a multimodal cognitive-behavioral approach: Results of a 3-year study. *Journal of Consulting and Clinical Psychology, 58*(4), 437–446.

Brophy, J. (1981). Teacher praise: A functional analysis. *Review of Educational Research, 51,* 5–32.

Brown, R., & Evans, W. P. (2002). Extracurricular activity and ethnicity: Creating greater school connection among diverse student populations. *Urban Education, 37*(1), 41–58.

Bryk, A. S., & Driscoll, M. E. (1988). *The school as community: Theoretical foundations, contextual influences, and consequences for students and teachers.* Madison: National Center on Effective Secondary Schools, University of Wisconsin.

Cameron, J., & Pierce, W. D. (1994). Reinforcement, reward, and intrinsic motivation: A meta-analysis. *Review of Educational Research, 64*(3), 363–423.

Cardenas, J. A., Montecel, M. R., Supik, J. D., & Harris, R. J. (1992). The Coca-Cola Valued Youth Program: Dropout prevention strategies for at-risk students. *Texas Researcher, 3,* 111–130.

Carnegie Council on Adolescent Development. (1989). *Turning points: Preparing American youth for the 21st century.* Washington, DC: Carnegie Corporation.

Catalano, R. F., Berglund, L. M., Ryan, J. A. M., Lonczak, H. S., & Hawkins, J. D. (2002). Positive youth development in the United States: Research findings on evaluations of positive youth development programs. *Prevention and Treatment, 5,* Article 15. Retrieved from http://www.journals.apa.org/prevention/volume5/toc-jun24-02.htm.

Catalano, R. F., & Hawkins, J. D. (2002). Response from authors to comments on "Positive youth development in the United States: Research findings on evaluations of positive youth development programs." *Prevention and Treatment 5,* Article 20. Retrieved from http://www.journals.apa.org/prevention/volume5/toc-jun24-02.htm.

Chisom, R., & Washington, M. (1997). *Undoing Racism: A Philosophy of International Social Change.* New Orleans, LA: The People's Institute Press.

Comer, J. P., Haynes, N. M., Joyner, E. T., & Ben-Avie, M. (Eds.). (1996). *Rallying the whole village: The Comer process for reforming education.* New York: Teachers College Press.

Connell, J. P., & Wellborn, J. G. (1991). Competence, autonomy, and relatedness: A motivational analysis of self-system processes. In M. R. Gunnar & L. S. Sroufe, (Eds.), *Self processes in development: Minnesota Symposium on Child Psychology,* Vol. 23 (pp. 43–77). Chicago: University of Chicago Press.

Cooperrider, D. L., Whitney, D., & Stavros, J. (2003). *Appreciative inquiry handbook: The first in a series of AI workbooks for leaders of change.* Cleveland, OH: Lakeshore Publishers.

Cotton, K. (1998). The academic and social effectiveness of small-scale schooling. *Journal of Early Education and Family Review,* 6(1), 25–28.

Covey, S. (1989). *The seven habits of highly effective people.* New York: Simon & Schuster.

Csikszentmihalyi, M. (1996). *Creativity: Flow and the psychology of discovery and invention.* New York: HarperCollins.

Darling-Hammond, L. (1996, March). The quiet revolution: Rethinking teacher development. *Educational Leadership, 53*(6), 4–10.

Deci, E. L., & Ryan, R. M. (1985). *Intrinsic motivation and self-determination in human behavior.* New York: Plenum.

Delpit, Lisa. (1995). *Other People's Children: Cultural Conflict in the Classroom.* New York: Morrow.

Denault, L. E. (1999). Restructuring? Keep it simple…consider looping! *Delta Kappa Gamma Bulletin, 65*(4), 19–26.

Drug Strategies. (1998). *Safe schools, safe students: A guide to violence prevention strategies.* Washington, DC, Author. Retrieved from http://www.drugstrategies.com.

Dryfoos, J. G. (1998). *Full-service schools.* San Francisco: Jossey-Bass.

Duckenfield, M., & Swanson, L. (1992). *Service-learning: Meeting the needs of youth at risk.* Clemson, SC: National Dropout Prevention Center.

Dusenbury, L. (1996) *Making the grade: A guide to school drug prevention programs.* Washington, DC: Drug Strategies.

Eccles, J., Wigfield, A., Midgley, C., Reuman, D., Mac Iver, D., & Feldlaufer, H. (1993). Negative effects of traditional middle schools on students' motivation. *Elementary School Journal, 93,* 553–574.

Elias, M. J., Weissberg, R. P., Hawkins, J. D., Perry, C. L., Zins, J. E., Dodge, K. A., Kendall, P. C., & Gottfredson, D. C. (1994). The school-based promotion of social competence: Theory, research, practice, and policy. In R. J. Haggerty, N. Garmezy, M. Rutter, & L. Sherrod (Eds.), *Stress, risk and resilience in children and adolescence: Processes, mechanisms, and interventions* (pp. 269–315). New York: Cambridge University Press.

Ellickson, P. L., & Bell, R. M. (1990). Drug prevention in junior high: A multi-site longitudinal test. *Science, 247,* 1299–1305.

Elmore, R. F. (2000). *Building a new structure for school leadership.* Washington, DC: Albert Shanker Institute.

Epstein, J. L. (1995). School/family/community partnerships: Caring for the children we share. *Phi Delta Kappan, 76,* 701–712.

Fein, R. A., Vossekuil, B., Pollack, W. S., Borum, R., Modzeleski, W., & Reddy, M. (2002). *Threat assessment in schools: A guide to managing threatening situations and to creating safe school climates.* Washington, DC: U.S. Department of Education and U.S. Secret Service. Retrieved from http://www.ed.gov/offices/OESE/SDFS.

Finn, J. D. (1993). *School engagement and students at risk.* Washington, DC: National Center for Education Statistics.

Frieberg, H. J. (1998). Measuring school climate: Let me count the ways. *Educational Leadership,* 56(1), 22–26.

Freiberg, H. J., Connell, M. L., & Lorentz, J. (2001). Effects of Consistency Management TM on student mathematics achievement in seven Chapter I elementary schools. *The Journal of Education for Students Placed at Risk, 6*(3) 249–270.

Gardner, H. (1993). *Multiple intelligences: The theory in practice.* New York: BasicBooks.

Goleman, D. (1995). *Emotional intelligence: Why it can matter more than IQ.* New York: Bantam Books.

Goodenow, C. (1993). Classroom belonging among early adolescent students: Relationships to motivation and achievement. *Journal of Early Adolescence, 13* (1), 21–43.

Gottfredson, D. C. (2001). *Schools and delinquency.* Cambridge, UK: Cambridge University Press.

Hawkins, J. D., Smith, B. H., & Catalano, R. F. (2004). Social development and social emotional learning. In J. E. Zins, R. P. Weissberg, M. C. Wang, & H. J. Walberg (Eds.), *Building academic success on social and emotional learning. What does the research say?* New York: Teachers College Press.

Henderson, A. T., & Berla, N. (1995). *A new generation of evidence: The family is critical to student achievement.* Washington, DC: Center for Law and Education.

Hilliard, A. (1991). Do we have the will to educate all children? *Educational Leadership, 49* (1), 31–36.

Hirschi, T. (1969). *Causes of delinquency.* Berkeley: University of California Press.

Holtz Frank, T. (1997, Winter). Guidelines for referring a student to counseling. *ALERT Educator,* 1–4. Retrieved from http://www.projectalert.com.

Holtz Frank, T. (2003, Fall). Creating community: A positive youth development program. *National Dropout Prevention Center/Network Newsletter.* Retrieved from http://www.mhric.org/cshw.

Jalloh, M., & Fuchs Nadeau, D. (2000). *Safe spaces: Creating safe and drug-free learning environments.* New Paltz: New York State Center for School Safety. Retrieved from http://www.mhric.org/scss.

Jenkins, J. E. (1996). The influence of peer affiliation and student activities on adolescent drug involvement. *Adolescence, 31,* 297–306.

Jessor, R., & Jessor, S. L. (1977). *Problem behavior and psychosocial development: A longitudinal study of youth.* New York: Academic Press.

Jessor, R., VanDenBos, J., Vanderryn, J., Costa, F. M., & Turbin, M.S. (1997). Protective factors in adolescent problem behavior: Moderator effects and developmental change. *Developmental Psychology, 31* (6), 923–933.

Johnson, D. W., & Johnson, R. T. (1999). *Learning together and alone: Cooperative, competitive, and individualistic learning.* Boston: Allyn & Bacon.

Klem, A. M., & Connell, J. P. (2004). Relationships matter: Linking teacher support to student engagement and achievement. *Journal of School Health, 74*(7), 262–273.

Kohl, H. (1994). *"I Won't Learn From You" and Other Thoughts on Creative Maladjustments.* New York: The New Press.

Kohn, A. (1996). *Beyond discipline: From compliance to community.* Alexandria, VA: ASCD.

Kouzes, J., & Posner, B. (2002). *The leadership challenge* (3rd ed.). San Francisco: Jossey-Bass.

Kozol, J. (1991). *Savage Inequalities: Children in America's Schools.* New York: Crown Publishers.

Kreidler, W. J. (1994). *Conflict resolution in the middle school: A curriculum and teaching guide.* Cambridge, MA: Educators for Social Responsibility.

Lee, V. E., Dedrick, R. F., & Smith, J. B. (1991). The effect of social organization of schools on teachers' efficacy and satisfaction. *Sociology of Education, 64*(3), 190–208.

Lee, V. E., & Smith, J. B. (1997). High school size: Which works best for whom? *Educational Evaluation and Policy Analysis, 19*(3), 205–228.

Lee, V. E., & Smith, J. B. (1999). Social support and achievement for young adolescents in Chicago: The role of the academic press. *American Educational Research Journal, 36*(4), 907–945.

Lewis, C. C., Schaps, E., & Watson, M. (1995). Beyond the pendulum: Creating challenging and caring schools. *Phi Delta Kappan, 76,* 547–554.

Little, J. W., & McLaughlin, M. W. (1993). *Teachers' work: Individuals, colleagues, and contexts.* New York: Teachers College Press.

LoSciuto, L., Rajala, A. K., Townsend, T. N., & Taylor, A. S. (1996). An outcome evaluation of Across Ages: An intergenerational mentoring approach to drug prevention. *Journal of Adolescent Research, 11*(1), 116–129.

Mac Iver, D. J. (1990). Meeting the needs of young adolescents: Advisory groups, interdisciplinary teaching teams, and school transition programs. *Phi Delta Kappan, 71*(6), 458–464.

Manlove, J. (1998). The influence of high school dropout and school disengagement on the risk of school-age pregnancy. *Journal of Research on Adolescence, 8*(2), 187–220.

Marzano, R. J., Pickering, D. J., & Pollock, J. E. (2001). *Classroom instruction that works.* Alexandria, VA: ASCD.

McFadden, A. C., Marsh, G. E., Price, B. J., & Hwang, Y. (1992). A study of race and gender bias in the punishment of school children. *Education and Treatment of Children, 15*(2), 140–146.

Meier, D. (1995). *The power of their ideas: Lessons for America from a small school in Harlem.* Boston: Beacon Press.

Metis Associates. (1990) *The Resolving Conflict Creatively program, 1988–1989: Summary of significant findings.* New York: Metis Associates.

Miller, J. B. (1976). *Toward a New Psychology of Women.* Boston: Beacon Press.

National Association of Secondary School Principals. (2004). *Breaking ranks II: Strategies for leading high school reform.* Reston, VA: Author.

Nettles, S. M., Mucherah, W., & Jones, D. S. (2000). Understanding resilience: The role of social resources. *Journal of Education for Students Placed at Risk, 5,* 47.

Noddings, N. (1992). *The challenge to care in schools: an alternative approach to education.* Advances in Contemporary Educational Thought Series; 8. New York: Teachers College Press.

Noguera, P. (2003). *City Schools and the American Dream.* New York: Teachers College Press.

Oakes, J., & Guiton, G. (1995). Teaming: Creating small communities of learners in middle grades. In J. Oakes & K. Hunter Quartz (Eds.), *Creating new educational communities* (pp. 87–107). Chicago: University of Chicago Press.

Olweus, D. (1993). *Bullying at school: What we know and what we can do.* New York: Blackwell.

Payne, Ruby. (1996). *A Framework for Understanding Poverty.* Texas:aha!process, Inc.

Perkins, P. G., & Milgram, R. B. (1996). Parental involvement in homework: A double-edge sword. *International Journal of Adolescence and Youth, 6*(3), 195–203.

Pittman, K. J., O'Brien, R., & Kimball, M. (1993). *Youth development and resiliency research: Making connections to substance abuse prevention.* Report prepared for The Center for Substance Abuse Prevention. Washington, DC: Center for Youth Development and Policy Research.

Pittman, K. J., & Wright, M. (1991). *Bridging the gap: A rationale for enhancing the role of community organizations promoting youth development.* Report prepared for The Task Force on Youth Development and Community Programs at the Carnegie Council on Adolescent Development. Washington, DC: Center for Youth Development and Policy Research.

Poliner, R. A., & Lieber, C. M. (2004). *The Advisory Guide: Designing and Implementing Effective Advisory Programs in Secondary Schools.* Cambridge, MA: Educators for Social Responsibility.

Resnick, M. D., Bearman, P. S., Blum, R. W., Bauman, K. E., Harris, K. M., Jones, J., Tabor, J., Beuhring, T., Sieving, R. E., Shew, M., Ireland, M., Bearinger, L. H., & Udry, J. R. (1997). Protecting adolescents from harm: Findings from the National Longitudinal Study on Adolescent Health. *Journal of the American Medical Association, 278,* 823–832.

Rutter, M. (1987). Psychosocial resilience and protective mechanisms. *American Journal of Orthopsychiatry, 57*(3), 316–331.

Ryan, A. M., & Patrick, H. (2001). The classroom social environment and changes in adolescents' motivation and engagement during middle school. *American Educational Research Journal, 38*(2), 437–460.

Sanders, M. G. (2001). The role of "community" in comprehensive school, family and community partnership programs. *Elementary School Journal, 102*(1), 19–34.

Schaps, E., Battistich, V., & Solomon, D. (1997). School as a caring community: A key to character education. In A. Molnar (Ed.), *The construction of children's character, part II: 96th yearbook of the National Society for the Study of Education.* Chicago: University of Chicago Press.

Schargel, F. P., & Smink, J. (2001). *Strategies to help solve our school dropout problem.* Larchmont, NY: Eye on Education.

Schinke, S. P. (1999). *Evaluation of Boys and Girls' Club of America's Educational Enhancement Program.* Atlanta, GA: Boys and Girls Clubs of America.

Schinke, S. P., Botvin, G. J., Trimble, J. E., Orlandi, M. A., Gilchrist, L. D., & Locklear, V. S. (1988). Preventing substance abuse among American-Indian adolescents: A bicultural competence skills approach. *Journal of Counseling Psychology, 35*(1), 87–90.

Schneider, T., Walker, H. M., & Sprague, J. R. (2000). *Safe school design: A handbook for educational leaders.* Eugene: ERIC Clearinghouse on Educational Management, College of Education, University of Oregon.

Schumacher, D. (1998). *The transition to middle school* (Report No. EDOPS-98-6). Washington, DC: Clearinghouse on Elementary and Early Childhood Education. (ERIC Document Reproduction Service No. ED 422 119)

Seidman, E., Aber, J. L., Allen, L., & French, S. E. (1996). The impact of the transition to high school on the self-system and perceived social context of poor urban youth. *American Journal of Community Psychology, 24,* 489–515.

Seligman, M. E. P. (1990). *Learned optimism.* New York: Pocket Books.

Senge, P. (1990). *The fifth discipline: The art and practice of the learning organization.* New York: Doubleday Currency.

Sergiovanni, T. J. (1994). *Building community in schools.* San Francisco: Jossey-Bass.

Sergiovanni, T. J. (1996). *Leadership for the schoolhouse.* San Francisco: Jossey-Bass.

Shumer, R. (1994). Community-based learning: Humanizing education. *Journal of Adolescence, 17*(4), 357–367.

Simons-Morton, B. G., & Crump, A. D. (2002). The association of parental involvement and social competence with school adjustment and engagement among sixth graders. *Journal of School Health, 73*(3), 121–126.

Skiba, R, & Peterson, R. (1999). The dark side of zero tolerance: Can punishment lead to safe schools? *Phi Delta Kappan, 80*(5), 372–76, 381–382.

Skinner, E. A., Wellborn, J. G., & Connell, J. P. (1990). What it takes to do well in school and whether I've got it: The role of perceived control in children's engagement and school achievement. *Journal of Educational Psychology, 82,* 22–32.

Slavin, R. E. (1991). Synthesis of research on cooperative learning. *Educational Leadership, 48*(5), 71–82.

Smylie, M. A. (1994). Redesigning teachers' work: Connections to the classroom. In L. Darling-Hammond (Ed.). *Review of research in education,* Vol. 20 (pp. 129–177). Washington, DC: American Educational Research Association.

Stevenson, C. (1992). *Teaching ten to fourteen year olds.* White Plains, N.Y: Longman.

Styles, D. (2001). *Class meetings: Building leadership, problem-solving and decision-making skills in the respectful classroom.* Markham, ON: Pembroke.

Sugai, G., Horner, R., & Gresham, F. (2001). Behaviorally effective school environments. In M. R. Shinn, G. Slover, & H. M. Walker (Eds.), *Interventions for academic and behavior problems.* Silver Spring, MD: National Association of School Psychologists.

Sugai, G., Sprague, J. R., Horner, R., Walker, H. M. (2001). Preventing school violence: The use of discipline referrals to assess and monitor schoolwide discipline interventions. *Journal of Emotional and Behavioral Disorders, 8*(2), 94–101.

Tatum, Beverly. (1991). *Why Are All the Black Kids Sitting Together? and Other Conversations about Race.* New York: Basic Books.

Tichy, N. M. with Cardwell, N. (2002). *The Cycle of Leadership. How Great Leaders Teach Their Companies to Win.* New York: Harper Business.

Tierney, J. P., Grossman, J. B., & Resch, N. L. (2000). *Making a difference: An impact study of Big Brothers/Big Sisters.* Philadelphia: Public/Private Ventures. Retrieved from http://www.ppv.org/ppv/publications/publications.asp?search_id=19.

U. S. Department of Education (1999). *Reducing class size: What do we know?* Washington DC: Author.

U.S. Department of Education, (2003). *When schools stay open late: The national evaluation of the 21st-Century Learning Centers program, first year findings.* Washington, DC: Author. Retrieved from http://www.ed.gov/pubs/21cent/firstyear.

U. S. Departments of Education and Justice (2000). *Early warning, timely response: A guide to safe schools.* Washington DC: Author.

Viadero, D. (1994). Learning to care. *Education Week, 13,* 31–33.

Voelkl, K. E. (1995). School warmth, student participation and achievement. *Journal of Experimental Education, 63,* 127–138.

Wasley, P. (2000). *Small schools, great strides: A study of new small schools in Chicago.* New York: Bank Street College of Education.

Waters. T., Marzano, R. J., & McNulty, B. A. (2003). *Balanced leadership: What 30 years of research tells us about the effects of leadership on achievement.* Aurora, CO: Mid-Continent Research for Education and Learning.

Wehlage, G. G., Rutter, R. A., Smith, G. A., Lesko, N., & Fernandez, R. R. (1989). *Reducing the risk: Schools as communities of support.* Philadelphia, Falmer Press.

Wellman, B., & Lipton, L. (2004). *Data-driven dialogue: A facilitator's guide to collaborative inquiry.* Sherman, CT: MiraVia.

Werner, E. E., & Smith, R. S. (1982). *Vulnerable but invincible: A longitudinal study of resilient children and youth.* New York: McGraw-Hill.

Werner, E. E., & Smith, R. S. (1992). *Overcoming the odds: High-risk children from birth to adulthood.* Ithaca, NY: Cornell University Press.

4

Establishing a Common Vision: Build It and They Will Come

What man can conceive and believe man can achieve.

Napoleon Hill

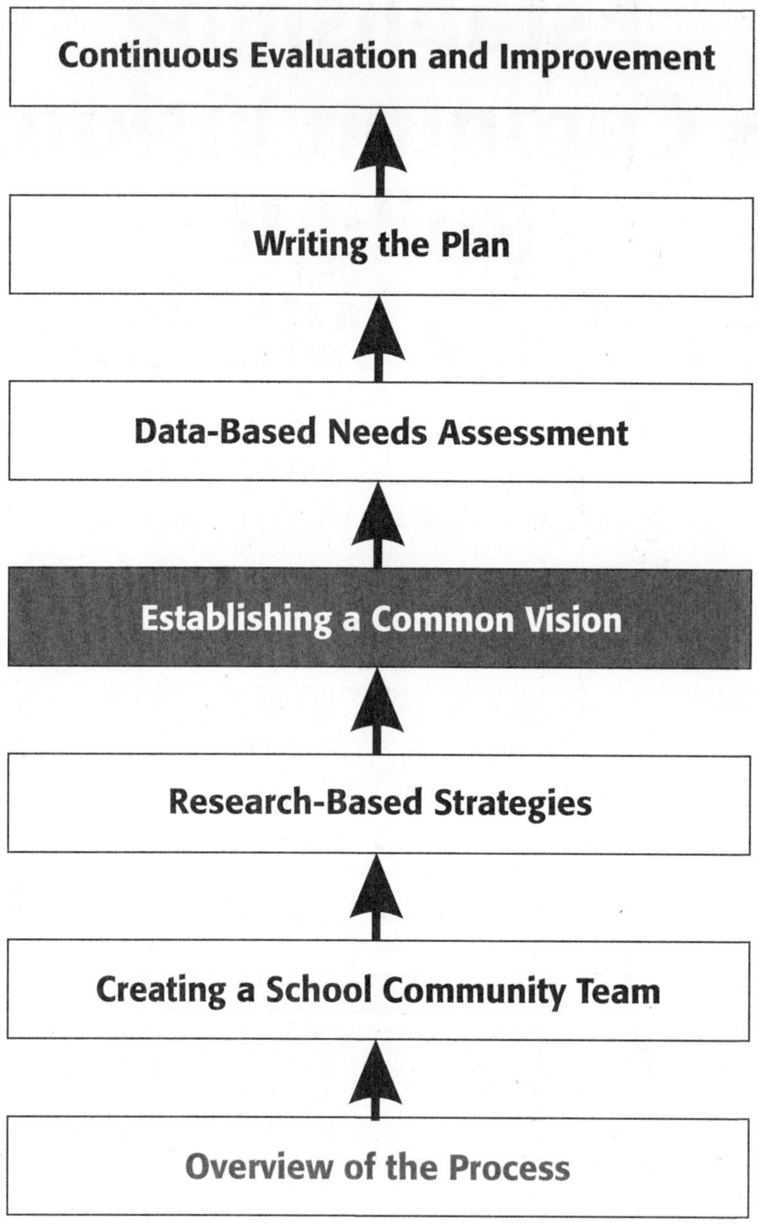
Continuous Evaluation and Improvement
Writing the Plan
Data-Based Needs Assessment
Establishing a Common Vision
Research-Based Strategies
Creating a School Community Team
Overview of the Process

Picture Success: A Vision of a Supportive Learning Environment

When I do schoolwide staff development sessions or classroom workshops with students on the theme of creating community and building supportive learning environments, I like to start with a series of questions:

- What do we mean by supportive learning environments?
- What are the students doing, the teachers, the principal, the parents, community members?
- What's happening in the hallways, the classrooms, and the cafeteria?

What's the feeling when a student, a parent, or a community member enters the building?

- What is the quality of the interaction between students and teachers, children and adult staff, teacher and teacher, school and family, or school and community members?
- What are the outcomes on student success and achievement, on teacher retention, on parent and community involvement, and on school improvement?

The answers are always revealing because they are generally the kinds of fundamental truths, hopes, and dreams that we all embrace.

Start with the Positive: A New Vision of School Improvement

Human systems grow in the direction of what they persistently ask questions about…The single most prolific thing a group can do if its aims are to liberate the human spirit and consciously construct a better future is to make the positive change core the common and explicit property of all.

David L. Cooperrider and Diana Whitney

The business of school improvement has been based mainly on a deficit model of thinking. We begin with the assumption that there is something wrong with the school that needs fixing. It starts with uncovering the problem, determining the root causes for the problem(s) and generating strategies to fix the school and the students. Underlying these assumptions are the unspoken beliefs that the people within the system are somehow flawed. This deficit thinking reflects most noticeably in our language. We speak of low-performing schools, of underperforming students, a lack of leadership at the administrative level, inadequate instructional practices, underqualified teachers, and on and on.

Is it any wonder that the school faculty, administrators, parents, and students are less than motivated to change and improve when we come in as the improvement team? It is clearly time to shift our thinking to new and creative ways to create environments that support all members as learners within the school community.

The process of envisioning a supportive learning environment begins by starting with the strengths of the system. How does one retrain and reframe thinking to look for the positive rather than the negative? We are accustomed as human beings to look for what is wrong rather than what is right. The old media adage "it if bleeds, it leads" is based on the theory that bad news sells. We have become a society of tragedy junkies and drama queens, feeding on other people's misfortunes. The voyeurism inherent in shows such as Jerry Springer and reality TV make a sad commentary on the state of our cultural values.

Yet, in the midst of this, there is a tremendous surge across our country and our world of activity, passion, and commitment to improve our schools, our environment, our workplaces, and the lives of people living in poverty around the globe. We see the emphasis on emotional intelligence valued along with traditional IQ. We hear about creativity, appreciative inquiry, social capitalism, and other driving forces that are taking their place in public and private discourse. We know that this energy of optimism, social consciousness, and empathy breeds greater motivation and is the hallmark of successful leaders, innovators, and creative thinkers (Seligman, 1990, 1994; Csikzentmihalyi, 1996; Goleman, 1995, 1998).

Building a positive environment begins with asking people to examine the strengths in the system; to remember past successes; to point to current examples of success or approximation of success. It asks people to remember moments and experiences of peak performance, of vitality, and excitement about the educational process; to remember the faces and names of the students who learned, who overcame obstacles, and who became successful despite the barriers. It builds resiliency and optimism throughout the system. This process is embedded in the visioning process described in this model, but it encompasses the worldview of participants in the entire improvement process itself.

Starting from this perspective does not mean ignoring areas in need of improvement. It simply means that the best way to motivate people and systems is to move them forward through a conscious process of discovering what is good and how to make it better. In fact, the very same tools of data analysis that are often used to discover the deficits can be used in this process. However, the quality of energy, motivation, and buy-in is substantially different when approached from an inherent belief in the wholeness of the system and the collective discovery of means for improvement.

Developing a Common Vision

Have you ever noticed that the return trip from an unfamiliar destination always seems shorter than the way there? After we know where we are going, the journey seems more manageable. The same is true for having an endpoint, a goal, a vision of where all our efforts and energy are leading. Without a vision, it's as if we are wandering aimlessly with no guideposts to let us know that we are progressing. In the absence of this positive feedback loop, the quarter-mile markers on the way up the mountain, it is easy for groups to become disillusioned and lose energy rapidly.

Vision is the best manifestation of creative imagination and the primary motivation of human action. It's the ability to see beyond our present reality, to create, to invent what does not yet exist, to become what we not yet are.

Stephen Covey

We have all had far more practice in the art of visioning than we may realize. The common childhood game of When I Grow Up and the adult version of When I Win the Lottery are actually exercises in the process of visualizing the desired outcome. The ability to think beyond the present, to project into the future and to imagine things not as they are, but as you wish them to be, takes practice and a fair amount of faith and confidence.

Visioning is the process of creating a vision or picture of a particular situation or event as the person desires it rather than how it appears in reality. Visioning requires projecting into the future and imagining how current events might evolve over time in the direction that one wants to go (that is, imagining the desired outcome in the future based on the current situation). *Vision statements* are the stated outcomes desired by the group or team. The vision statement reflects a shared consensus and agreement that the group collectively seeks the same outcome and that members agree about the nature of what that outcome will look like.

Some significant features of the visioning process distinguish it from related activities such as wishing, hoping, and dreaming. Terms such as visioning, visualization, or vision statements might sound vaguely familiar. To clarify, let us look at some simple distinctions.

How Is Visioning Different from Dreaming?

The process of visioning requires a disciplined approach. It requires self-examination, practice, and belief. It demands reciprocity: In exchange for the realization of the vision, you must commit to expending energy to achieve your goals.

Dreaming, however, is usually a pleasurable activity that involves no real commitment on the part of the individual. Although one might dream, wish, and hope for something wonderful to happen, there is no real plan or even a firm belief that the outcome will occur. It remains solely in the realm of fantasy, wishful thinking, and bears little resemblance to the kind of concentrated effort required to envision real goals and aspirations. As they say, "Dream in one hand, spit in the other. Which fills up faster?"

When one engages in a visioning process, it is a conscious act of creation rather than an idle pastime. This distinction is particularly relevant when confronting people who feel that the process of visioning is a waste of time, and would rather marginalize it as nothing more than daydreaming.

The Power of Visualizing

Research in peak performance (Csikszentimihalyi, 1996) shows that star performers—whether they are Olympic athletes, top sales managers, artists, or NASA astronauts—are involved in the process of visioning or visualizing. In this sense, visualizing becomes practice for training the mind to expect success, rather than simply rehearsing the specific actions involved in performance. When visualizing, one goes beyond the memorization of precise movements and extends into the realm of imagined success, outpacing one's opponents in a competition, or—in the case of peak performance learning environments—perhaps seeing the smiling faces of young people; the school filled with productive, busy, and successful students; parents actively engaged in education; and the community alive with activity.

Visioning is tied to success in every endeavor that involves people—from business, to sports, to creating programs and organizational structures. It is therefore critical to gain agreement and active involvement from the group in forming a coherent vision statement.

Benefits of Visioning

- Trains the mind to expect success
- Creates optimism and energy
- Engages the group in a creative process
- Creates collective commitment and buy-in
- Provides a focus for group efforts
- Forms the foundation for the project or endeavor
- Develops motivation and ownership of group success
- Accesses new and innovative ideas and ways of thinking
- Teaches valuable life skills for success

Jump Start Your Personal Vision

Visualization, the act of imagining the desired outcome, is a skill that requires practice. It is important to create vivid visual pictures and imagery in your mind so you can truly see what you want to achieve. It is equally important to imbue these pictures with strong emotional content, given that the subconscious mind relates on the visual and emotional levels. The idea is to imbed your vision deeply into both your conscious and subconscious mind, your left and right hemispheres of the brain. This technique, sometimes referred to as *imprinting,* is a creative process as much as an intellectual one.

Tips for Personal Visualization

- Identify personally with the images you create by injecting yourself into the picture.
- Create a clear and well-defined image including the Who, What, Where, When, and How of the events pictured.
- Generate as much positive emotion as possible and associate that emotion with the picture in your mind.
- Include positive affirmations or self-statements that describe the benefits you will derive from achieving this goal.

Getting Buy-In, or Whose Big Idea Was This Anyway?

Active involvement is the key to meaningful participation, which in turn increases motivation and buy-in. It is vital to have a participatory process that encourages each member to share thoughts and ideas, and allows for different forms of contribution to each—according to personal strengths. The exercises outlined in this section ensure that the vision created by the group comes from the group rather than from a single member or imposed on the group from an outside agent or authority. Even if there is a mandate involved in the project, such as an external funder, the group must assume control of the process, the vision, and the act of creating a solid plan to sustain their efforts through the inevitable obstacles and achieve success.

What to Do If a Member Consistently Interferes with the Process

During this process, groups are likely to encounter resistance from members. At every phase of the planning process, there might be members who feel threatened and experience fear—fear of change, fear of challenging themselves to think and act in new and different ways, fear that being open-minded might shake their world view.

This resistance can surface in the form of skeptical or sarcastic comments designed to distract attention from the act of creating, dreaming, and thinking larger than life. Comments might include "This is a waste of time," or "Get real—this isn't ever going to happen." People who engage in this behavior, sometimes referred to as dream stealers or vision killers, have created habits and patterns of negative thinking, and might find it very difficult to change.

Unfortunately, the saying is quite true that one rotten apple spoils the whole barrel. Negativity, like positivity, is contagious. The group needs to develop guidelines for creating a safe environment. These guidelines can serve to minimize disruptions and decrease the open expressions of negativity. To ensure the integrity of the process, it is important that members display proactive and respectful behavior toward each other and toward the aims of the group. A willingness to adhere to the basic ground rules in the planning process is a prerequisite for continued participation.

The group can't afford to ignore a member who is consistently negative and derisive toward the process and other members. Members who continue this behavior should be asked to sit the process out. Nonparticipating, or passing, is an option, but poisoning the group environment is not. It is seen as a violation of group norms and practices, which interferes with the group's ability to function.

If disruptions and negativity persist, consider asking the member to delay becoming involved until the initiative is more fully formed or, as a last resort, to leave. Use a skillful, gentle interaction between the negative member and a facilitator or small group of members. You might say the following: "You seem unhappy with the process we are going through. Your behavior is interfering with other members' abilities to be a full part of this process. Are you willing to adhere to our guidelines? If not, if this makes you too uncomfortable, perhaps you would prefer to participate later on rather than be part of the planning." Although the concept of having to remove a disruptive member might be distasteful, particularly to groups struggling to be inclusive and to attract members, it is ultimately the only way to ensure the integrity of both the process and the group. A few committed members can accomplish a lot more than 10 or 20 unmotivated or negative members.

Creating a Safe Environment for Sharing

An important first step in this phase of the process is gaining agreements around a few simple ground rules that will allow everyone to feel safe and comfortable when sharing. Talking about what one deeply desires, even in the context of professional or civic work, can be very exposing and therefore quite threatening to people unused to or uncomfortable with that level of sharing.

Have a member act as a facilitator and ask the group what they need from others to feel safe enough to share thoughts and ideas. Record the responses on a flip chart and use them for future meetings. To ensure input from a wide cross-section of members rather than a few dominant members, try to reach a consensus by asking, "Does everyone agree with this? Are there any other ideas or suggestions?" Techniques such as round robin or going around in a circle ensure equal participation.

Sample agreements or ground rules include respecting what others say, attempting to be nonjudgmental, listening to others, trying to understand what others are saying before responding, and trying to respond instead of reacting. Gaining agreement up front can minimize resistance later on. If negative comments or attitudes do surface, members can are simply reminded of the ground rules.

Another important component is to have a strong facilitator who can model the process, someone who inspires respect and can exemplify the qualities of an open and respectful communicator. By sharing a personal vision, the facilitator can often make it safer for others to share as well.

The facilitator does not have to hold any formal position of authority within the school. Instead, it is helpful to find people within the school and community who have informal power and are well-respected. Having someone other than the formal leader—a teacher, a social worker, or a community person—facilitate or cofacilitate can help share power. This sends an important message from the start that the process will be equitable and invites open participation and involvement from all members.

Difference Between a Vision Statement and a Mission Statement

The major difference between a mission and vision statement is that a mission statement is present tense, and a vision statement projects into the future. The vision creates a compelling picture of what can be—what's possible.

Vision	Mission
Future tense	Present tense
Long-term goals	Current goals
What you strive to attain, which is slightly out of reach right now	What you strive to become
What are your ultimate goals?	What do you intend to accomplish?
What is your driving force or reason for being?	What is your purpose?
What can you ultimately accomplish?	What do you do?
For whom can you do it?	For whom do you do it?
How will the future look?	What is the benefit?
Sample Vision Statement	Sample Mission Statement
"Our vision is to create a school that is highly regarded for its academic excellence and for its contribution to actively serving and improving the community in which it operates."	"By providing quality education, we empower individuals to become caring, competent, responsible citizens who value education as a lifelong process."

Tips for Developing a Vision Statement

After you engage in one of the strategies described in the figures in this chapter, define your vision statement with one or two clear statements or a series of statements. Do not get lost in rhetoric or jargon. Instead, move through the process until there is clarity for exactly what the group is attempting to accomplish.

- Get input from the group for developing a collective vision
- Dream the impossible dream of what can be rather than what is
- Create clear, compelling descriptions
- Identify common themes
- Identify key phrases
- Draft a vision statement
- Submit it to students, staff, and families for revision
- Revise based on feedback
- Develop a timeline for completion

Picture Success: Vision Statements

Here are sample vision statements from a wide cross-section of industries and enterprises. Note that some are simple statements, whereas others are paragraphs.

> *Land a man on the moon and safely return him to earth by the end of this decade.*
>
> John F. Kennedy

Famous challenge issued to NASA in 1961.

> *I have a dream that my four children will one day live in a nation where they will not be judged by the color of their skin but by the content of their character.*
>
> Martin Luther King

An excerpt from the famous "I Have a Dream" speech, spoken at the conclusion of the Civil Rights March on Washington, 1968

> *Healthy people in a healthy world.*
>
> Centers for Disease Control

> *To become the most competitive enterprise in the world by being number one or number two in market share in every business the company is in.*
>
> Jack Welch, General Electric

Famous challenge that CEO Jack Welch issued to his division heads in the mid-1980s.

> *Year after year, Westin and its people will be regarded as the best and most sought-after hotel and resort management group in North America.*
>
> Westin Hotels

References

Cooperrider, D. L., Whitney, D., & Stavros, J. (2003). *Appreciative inquiry handbook: The first in a series of AI workbooks for leaders of change.* Cleveland, OH: Lakeshore Publishers.

Covey, S. (1989). *The seven habits of highly effective people.* New York: Simon & Schuster.

Csikszentmihalyi, M. (1996). *Creativity: flow and the psychology of discovery and invention.* New York: HarperCollins.

Goleman, D. (1995). *Emotional intelligence: Why it can matter more than IQ.* New York: Bantam Books.

Goleman, D. (1998). *Working with emotional intelligence.* New York: Bantam Books.

Seligman, M. E. P. (1990). *Learned optimism.* New York: Pocket Books

Seligman, M. E. P. (1994). *What you can change and what you can't.* New York: Knopf.

Figure 4.1. Create a News Article for a Future Program

Exercise 1: Create a news article featuring your program with a date three years from now.
NEWS FLASH! **A SUCCESS STORY:** **CREATING COMMUNITY CREATES A WHOLE LOT MORE** Over the past three years, __________ has seen dramatic changes in its school and community because of its supportive learning environment program, Creating Community. Nowadays, a visitor to the _________ community is likely to notice...

Create a few positive descriptions of your vision of a supportive learning environment that involves any of the following factors: cooperative learning in small groups taking place in the classrooms, with computers, student art work and recognition awards lining the hallways; sense of pride of accomplishments; significant gains in student achievement; role of the principal as organizational leader, teacher, and learner; high staff morale; innovative staff development programs in providing performance feedback, managing diversity, enhancing conflict resolution, and providing stress-reduction skills for home and work; respectful student/staff interaction; welcome centers and buddy programs for incoming students and their families; positive and supportive interactions among students; high school helpers as cross-age tutors, peer facilitators and mentors; advisory groups; students facilitating open classroom discussions; afterschool programs; student service learning projects in the school or community; community members involved in fundraising, apprenticeship, and mentoring programs; parents running a Parent Center in the school or community to welcome new parents, provide parenting education, and so on.

Use the different senses to paint the picture of your vision, such as a feeling of, the sounds of, and the sight of the vision. Use imaginary quotes from students, staff, teachers, administrators, parents, and community members.

Figure 4.2. Guiding Questions for Developing a Vision

- What are the strengths in our learning community right now?
- What are examples of past successes?
- What are peak experiences we have had in helping another person learn?
- What are peak experiences we have had in developing vital learning communities at home, in the community, in the classroom, in the school?
- If we could make the impossible possible with this program, what do we really want to do for the people within our learning community by developing this program?
- How does what we see for our project enhance or expand what we are already doing?
- What would it look like in our wildest dreams?
- If money were no object, what would we like to accomplish with this program?
- How would we know we have been successful?

Figure 4.3.

Exercise 2: Dyadic Interview
Conduct a dialogue between two people using the guiding questions from Figure 4.2. Allow each person to speak uninterrupted for a full 10 minutes. The listener takes notes. When the speaker is done, the listener will speak for one to two minutes and feed back what they heard the speaker say. The speaker may then take one minute to clarify or add any additional details. Switch places. The listener now becomes the speaker. Repeat the process.

Exercise 3: Guided Interview

1. Use the guiding questions from Figure 4.2.
2. Conduct this exercise as an individual interview in groups of three. One person functions as the interviewer/facilitator, one functions as the scribe, and one is the interviewee. Take turns until each person has had a chance to answer the guiding questions.
3. Compare notes first in your small triad. Divide a sheet of flip chart paper down the middle and fill in one side as Common Themes and one side as Unique Features.
4. Create a sheet on a flip chart with the same two columns: Common Themes and Unique Features.
5. Go around and have each triad list one item for each column from their list until the lists are exhausted.
6. Appoint a skilled facilitator for this part of the process who can point out, along with the group, the same items repeated by various groups and then consolidate these items to form a more concise, cohesive list. It is important not to rush this part of the process. It may take some time to whittle down the items into three or four major themes.
7. Have the group form the items into a consolidated vision statement. Be careful to keep the full flavor or intention of the group while crafting a sentence and not get lost in jargon.

Figure 4.4.

Exercise 4: Creative Arts Expressions: Project Success
Use the guiding questions from Figure 4.2. The end product of these questions can be a visual image such as a drawing, a symbol, or a mandala. It can be a written description, such as a poem, an essay, a short story, a letter, or a news column. It can be a conversation with a friend or group member. It can take the form of a real or scripted audiotaped interview. It can be a graph or chart that illustrates the sequence by denoting the beginning and end points. It can also be any other technique you might feel comfortable using. Allow this to be a fully open, exploratory process that holds personal meaning and provides a mechanism to communicate the end product with others to engage them later in the process.

Figure 4.5.

Exercise 5: Sculpture: Project Success
Divide into smaller groups and have each team devise a sculptural representation of the project using Legos, Tinkertoys, or Playdoh.

Figure 4.6.

Exercise 6: Documentary: Project Success
Use the guiding questions from Figure 4.2 (page 108). ▪ Write or draw the story line. ▪ Identify the main characters. ▪ Write or draw a synopsis of the plot. ▪ How does the story end? ▪ Videotape, audiotape, or film the story.

Figure 4.7.

Exercise 7: Board Game: Project Success
Object of the game: For as many team members as possible to successfully reach the finish line (goal) without being lost or devoured along the way. **Description:** Using the guiding questions from Figure 4.2, create a board game with pictures and symbols for the start of the journey, the adventures along the way, any obstacles or barriers, and the end goal. **Materials:** Draw a game board on cardboard. Use pieces for the players made from clay or paper, or found objects such as corks and bottle caps to symbolize the members of the team. Have a set of dice or some kind of spinner to indicate the number of spaces players can progress. **Other ideas:** Use the game with families and invite them to a family game night. Use it as part of a staff development session. Use it with students as part of a leadership class.

5

Conducting Data-Based Needs Assessment: Get Real!

I have not failed. I've just found 10,000 ways that won't work.

Thomas Alva Edison

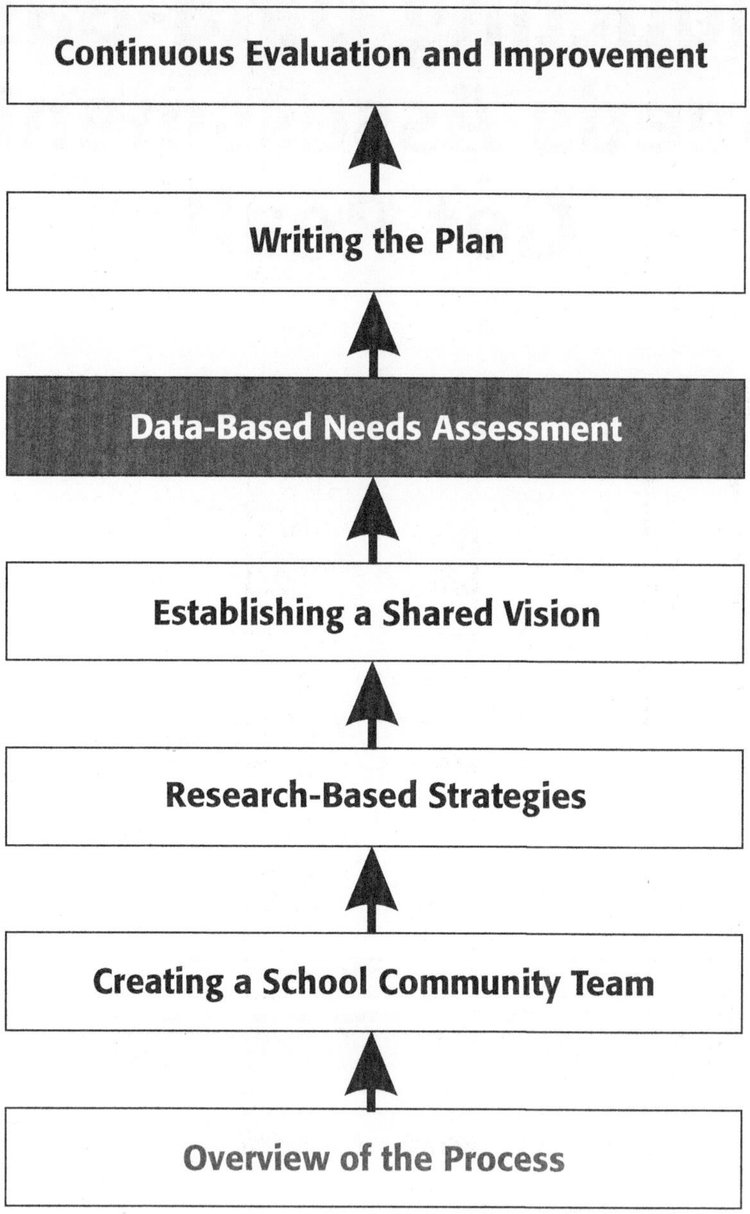
Continuous Evaluation and Improvement
Writing the Plan
Data-Based Needs Assessment
Establishing a Shared Vision
Research-Based Strategies
Creating a School Community Team
Overview of the Process

Four Phases of the Needs Assessment Process
▪ Phase One: Refocus on the Vision ▪ Phase Two: Engage in an Exploratory Discussion ▪ Phase Three: Collect Multiple Indicators and Data Sources ▪ Phase Four: Uncover the Needs through Data

Overview of the Needs Assessment Process

The needs assessment process is designed to point the way toward accurate problem solving. The team needs to know that it is focusing on the proper areas for the right reasons. A careful data analysis allows the team to pinpoint the target of its interventions and to make wise use of existing resources. It provides the answers to what is working well (and for whom) and what is not working well within the school.

These areas are initially explored through a thoughtful discussion of the current picture of student achievement and the factors that influence the learning environment. The team examines its underlying assumptions and intuitive hunches and then generates further questions about the current situation.

Multiple sources of data and corresponding indicators are collected and examined to determine negative and positive trends, patterns, and gaps. Areas of strength and existing assets are identified. Problem areas that require immediate attention are prioritized.

No Short-Term Fixes

Schools frequently use programs to solve problems. Without proper forethought and planning, these programs can often cause more harm than good, however. The tough work of sifting through the data and underlying assumptions can be bypassed by teams looking for an immediate solution. These short-term fixes are invariably short-lived, are nonsustainable, and do nothing to create systemic improvement. At best, they can ameliorate symptoms. At worst, they can be damaging to morale and can hamper involvement efforts.

Because staff, students, family, and community members have repeatedly experienced the school's disease-of-the-month and corresponding strategy-of-the-month syndromes, they might have a jaded attitude of been there, done that the next time school improvement is mentioned.

The other side of the coin, of course, is engaging in paralysis by analysis through embarking on endless commissions to study the problem without ever getting to the action stage. Clearly, a well-thought-out needs assessment process should lead to explicit and concise actions on the part of the team. These actions, selected by the team after careful study, are those evidence-based practices considered to be the most likely to support student learning.

Phase One: Refocus on the Vision

Guide the group to restate the vision. (See the following refocusing activities.)

Start with Your Strengths

Most of what we read or see on television is bad news. We rarely read reports of the many kind and caring acts engaged in by our fellow human beings. It seems as if we have been taught to find the flaws rather than the beauty in others and ourselves. Yet almost all of us intuitively respond to a beautiful sunset, a striking piece of art, the adorable face of an infant cradled in her mother's arms. These responses are sometimes conditioned out of us as we are taught to focus on what we get wrong, not what we get right.

Groups can begin the problem-solving process by looking at what is not working. Moving away from the deficit model takes constant vigilance and discipline because in the initial stages the group will invariably continue to focus on the flaws or insufficiencies of the system. This negative focus can result in feelings of hopelessness or being overwhelmed, and a loss of vital energy.

Appreciation of what is good in the world requires learning a new set of skills. The group needs to be directed to focus on its strengths, not just its weaknesses. Maintaining an appreciative lens can establish the momentum for positive change, which can reinvigorate the group and lead the way toward planning for success.

Guide the group to restate the vision (refer to Chapter 4). Each member should be able to state the vision in personal terms. Keep a printed copy of the collective vision in sight at all times. Ask group members to keep the picture of the vision uppermost in their minds at all times.

Emphasis should be on areas of strength as well as on areas for improvement. Trying to keep a balance between the two will be the job of the group as it delves into the difficult arena of the specific areas that need improvement. Check to see whether the group is beginning to veer into a negative, deficit-ridden approach. Beginning groups can be more vulnerable to this and might require additional coaching, facilitation, and external structures or protocols. Gently redirect the members, reminding them that this process is driven by appreciating strengths as well as being realistic about areas for improvement. Use energizing activities, stress breaks, or specific learning tools to refresh the process and reframe the discussion in a more positive and optimistic direction.

Refocus on the Vision

Picture Success: Refocusing Activities to Enhance Needs Assessment Discussions

- Brainstorm or conduct a round robin around a word or phrase such as "community," "vision," "supportive learning environment," "school improvement," or "shared learning." Choose a member to record the group's responses on a flip chart.
- Conduct the same activity: Invite participants to draw a symbol or picture that represents the word or term. Share as pairs and quartets; then in a large group, if time allows.
- Display a visual image or photograph and ask groups to respond to it in light of the key word or term. Have participants respond in pairs, in small groups, or as a large group. (You can find terrific images—such as nature scenes, or people engaged in fishing, running, or other activities—on the Internet.)
- Introduce written text that might be relevant or serve as a written example of successful practices in other schools. Conduct paired learning activities in which partners share their impressions of the reading with each other and then in smaller groups. The small groups can then distill their ideas down to a single phrase or sentence to share with the large group.

Figure 5.1. Generating Questions and Data Sources: What's Working?

Personal Observations: What do you think is currently going well in the school?	
Hypothesis/Causal Analysis: Why do you think these things are going well? What are the factors causing this?	
Assumptions: What assumptions are you basing your hypothesis on?	
Questions: What questions do you need to ask to find out if your hypothesis is true?	
Data Sources: What data sources would you need to answer your questions?	

Figure 5.2. Generating Questions and Data Sources: What's Not Working?

Personal Observations: What do you think are currently some specific areas for improvement in the school?	
Hypothesis/Causal Analysis: Why do you think these areas are not going well? What are the factors causing this?	
Assumptions: What assumptions are you basing your hypothesis on?	
Questions: What questions do you need to ask to find out if your hypothesis is true?	
Data Sources: What data sources would you need to answer your questions?	

Phase Two: Engage in an Exploratory Discussion

A helpful protocol to use at this time is to require all members to ask questions rather than make statements (see Figures 5.1, page 118 and 5.2, page 119).

Questions Before Answers

Our data are only as good as the questions we ask. A helpful protocol to use at this time is to require all members to ask questions rather than make statements. The questions then generate a need to move beyond surface data and seek out additional data sources. The team can generate a series of questions that they want discussed during these discussions. This will help engage the group in the spirit of active curiosity and discovery rather than allowing the strong and passionate opinions of a few to lock the group into certain explanations and modes of thinking. It also lays the groundwork for examining multiple data sources and indicators of student success before jumping to any set conclusions.

Prior to looking at data, team participants can engage in a discussion to share their personal observations, hypotheses, underlying assumptions, and questions. Initially, members share personal observations about what they feel is working well in the school. (This discussion will flow naturally from the restatement of the vision and the refocusing activities outlined previously.) They then generate their hypothesis and analyze causal factors by answering the following questions: Why? Why do you think this is happening?

At this point, members are asked to surface the underlying assumptions they are using to color their hypothesis. This is an important point because it allows open discussion about what lenses or filters members are using to view their world. It emphasizes the fact that they are looking through their own particular perspective and expands the possibilities of entertaining other perspectives. In distinguishing between hypotheses and assumptions, members come to understand that they are simply guesses, not facts; they illuminate subjective reality, not objective reality.

Exercise: Generating Questions and Data Sources

Use the worksheets from Figures 5.1 and 5.2 for this process. It is recommended that this process be conducted in the following way:

1. Members complete the worksheets individually. Be sure to start with Figure 5.1 (what is working well) before moving to Figure 5.2 (areas for improvement).
2. Divide the group into pairs; members take turns sharing their lists. Again, begin with Figure 5.1 before moving to Figure 5.2.
3. The pairs write only their questions on a sheet of flip chart paper.
4. The pairs write their data sources on a separate piece of chart paper.
5. Each pair takes turns reading the questions to the large group.
6. The group starts with the first pair who reads the data sources. Each subsequent group crosses out any duplication until all data sources are listed.
7. The chart paper showing Questions and Data Sources should be saved (or transferred into a Word document) for future discussions.

Phase Three: Collect Multiple Data Sources and Indicators

Figures 5.3 (page 122) and 5.4 (page 125) show multiple indicators and data sources with a checklist for use.

Figure 5.3. Multiple Indicators and Data Sources

1. Collect multiple sources of data and examine data as indicators to determine positive and negative patterns, trends, and gaps.
2. Disaggregate data by race, socioeconomic status, ethnicity, English language learners, special education, disability, gender, age, grade level, and months and years in the school. For parents/guardians, include level of educational attainment and if residing with child.

Data Source	Type of Data	Questions to Ask
Discipline records	Referrals; detention, in-school and out-of-school suspensions, expulsions, referrals for counseling, referrals for mandatory service by youth.	▪ Type of incident? (Specific infraction) ▪ Who is involved? (Students) ▪ Where? (Location) ▪ When? (Time of day, month, year) ▪ Causes? (External and internal factors) ▪ By whom? (Staff making referrals)
Uniform Violent Incident Reports (UVIRs)	Mandated UVIR data for infractions that qualify as violent.	▪ Type of incident? (Specific infraction) ▪ Who is involved? (Students) ▪ Where? (Location) ▪ When? (Time of day, month, year) ▪ Causes? (External and internal factors) ▪ By whom? (Staff making referrals)
Attendance	Excused and unexcused daily absences; incidents of tardiness, cutting classes, cutting school. Attendance in extracurricular activities.	▪ Is student cutting classes? ▪ Is student late to class? Late to school? ▪ Which classes? ▪ Which days of the week? ▪ Which months of the year? ▪ What about excused absences? ▪ Which students attend which extracurricular activities?

Data Source	Type of Data	Questions to Ask
School completion rates	Actual numbers of students entering middle school and high school, and actual numbers completing each grade level, accounting for relocating families moving into and out of the district.	▪ Which and how many students are entering? Graduating? Not graduating? At 8th grade? 9th? 10th? 11th? 12th? ▪ Compare same cohorts 8th to 12th grade. ▪ Who are the newly arrived students and at which grade level? Relocated students?
Achievement and achievement gaps	Achievement by population, grade levels, report cards, regent scores, state assessments, tests, and teacher reports, by percentile.	▪ Who is achieving at what percentile? ▪ In what subject areas? ▪ With which teachers? ▪ What and where are the disparities in student achievement?
School report card	Schoolwide achievement. School populations.	▪ What does this tell us about who is achieving, and in what?
Student surveys	Survey tools.	▪ What can students tell us about their thoughts and feelings about the school?
Parent and staff surveys	Survey tools.	▪ What do parents and staff say about the school?
Parent involvement	Phone contacts, visits, attendance at meetings, written correspondence.	▪ Who are the involved parents? ▪ Who are the uninvolved parents? ▪ How are parents involved in the school? ▪ Which parents are involved in what?
Community involvement	Partnership agreements, utilization rates for services, attendance at meetings.	▪ Who in the community is involved in the school? How? ▪ Who in the community is not involved?
Support services and resources for students and families	List existing services. Include in-school and out-of-school resources such as extracurricular activities; afterschool programs; and medical, mental health, arts enrichment, and community services.	▪ What services are available? ▪ Who is using the services? (Students, families) ▪ When and how frequently? ▪ Who is making the referrals? ▪ Which staff? ▪ What services are not being used?

Data Source	Type of Data	Questions to Ask
Department of Social Services	Supplemental aid to families. Food stamps. Disability insurance. Homeless population.	▪ How many families are receiving social services? ▪ What types of services? ▪ Who is homeless?
Free and reduced lunch data	School records for reduced and free lunch.	▪ What percentage of the population receives free and reduced lunch?
Census data	Related to race, ethnicity, newly arrived immigrants, poverty, and economic status in the community.	▪ Who is in our community? ▪ How has it changed?
Criminal justice data	Incidence of crime in the community; records of victims, prison population, potential indicator of children of incarcerated parents.	▪ What is the crime rate? ▪ In what neighborhoods? ▪ Who are the victims? ▪ What is the prison population? ▪ How many children have incarcerated parents?
Department of Health epidemiological data	Incidence of HIV/AIDS, possible indicators of children of parents living with chronic disease, and sexually transmitted diseases.	▪ What is the rate of HIV infections? ▪ What is the rate of babies who are born HIV+? ▪ What is the rate of sexually transmitted diseases?
Chamber of Commerce	Records of existing businesses.	▪ What type and how many businesses exist in the community? ▪ Which incentives are offered to businesses?
Real estate records	Property values, tax assessments.	▪ What is the average value of a home? ▪ In what neighborhood? ▪ How much does the school receive annually through property taxes?

Figure 5.4. Multiple Indicators and Data Sources Worksheet

1. List the multiple sources of data collected and examine data as indicators to determine positive and negative patterns, trends, and gaps.
2. Disaggregate data by race, socioeconomic status, ethnicity, English language learners, special education, disability, gender, age, grade level, and months and years in the school. For parents/guardians, include level of educational attainment and whether residing with child.

Data Source	Type of Data Collected	Questions to Ask
Discipline records		■ Type of incident? (Specific infraction) ■ Who is involved? (Students)Where? (Location) ■ When? (Time of day, month, year) ■ Causes? (External and internal factors) ■ By whom? (Staff making referrals)
Uniform Violent Incident Reports (UVIRs)		■ Type of incident? (Specific infraction)? ■ Who is involved? (Students)Where? (Location)? ■ When? (Time of day, month, year)? ■ Causes? (External and internal factors) ■ By who? (staff making referrals)?
Attendance		■ Is student cutting classes? ■ Is student late to class? Late to school? ■ Which classes? ■ Which days of the week? ■ Which months of the year? ■ What about excused absences? ■ Which students attend which extracurricular activities?
School completion rates		■ Which and how many students are entering? Graduating? Not graduating? At 8th grade? 9th? 10th? 11th? 12th? ■ Compare same cohorts 8th—12th grade. ■ Which and who are the newly arrived students and at which grade level? ■ Relocated students?

Data Source	Type of Data Collected	Questions to Ask
Achievement and achievement gaps		■ Who is achieving at what percentile? ■ In what subject areas? ■ With which teachers? ■ What and where are the disparities in student achievement?
School report card		■ What does this tell us about who is achieving and in what?
Student surveys		■ What can students tell us about their thoughts and feelings about the school?
Parent and staff surveys		■ What do parents and staff have to say about the school?
Parent involvement		■ Who are the involved parents? ■ Who are the uninvolved parents? ■ How are parents involved in the school? ■ Which parents are involved in which school activities?
Community involvement		■ Who in the community is involved in the school? ■ How? ■ Who in the community is not involved?
Support services and resources for students and families		■ What services are available? ■ Who is using the services? (Students, families) ■ When and how frequently? ■ Who is making the referrals? (Which staff in the school) ■ What services are not being used?
Department of Social Services		■ How many families are receiving social services? ■ What types of services? ■ Who is homeless?
Free and reduced lunch data		■ What percentage of the population receives free and reduced lunch?
Census data		■ Who is in our community? ■ How has it changed
Criminal justice data		■ What is the crime rate? ■ In what neighborhoods? ■ Who are the victims? ■ What is the prison population? ■ How many children have incarcerated parents?

Data Source	Type of Data Collected	Questions to Ask
Department of Health epidemiological data		■ What is the rate of HIV infections? ■ What is the rate of babies who are born HIV+? ■ What is the rate of sexually transmitted diseases?
Chamber of Commerce data		■ What types and how many businesses exist in the community? ■ What incentives are offered to businesses?
Real estate records		■ What is the average value of a home? ■ In what neighborhood? ■ How much does the school receive annually through property taxes?

Diverse Data Sources

Team members are now ready to begin collecting data. The team needs to ask these questions: How can we uncover additional information? Whom should we ask that we have not yet asked (students, staff, parents, community members)? Where have we not yet looked?

Often, schools are operating with only part of the picture because information is missing from key stakeholders about key issues. Many times, the mistaken notion is that all data are being considered—when in fact, insufficient data has been collected. This is often the result of an overemphasis on academics and an underemphasis on other aspects of the learning community. Generating additional data sources is an important step toward opening up the conversation, widening the lens through which teams are looking, and becoming more inclusive of the entire school community.

Find the most likely people and places to gather the specific forms of data and create an action item for the next agenda—Collect Data—listing the name of the person(s) responsible for reporting back the information.

Once again, a diverse team is in an ideal position to collect multiple sources of data based on who may have the best access to various sources. Members of the business community may be in an ideal position to gain access to business and real estate-related data, health professionals may be better suited to gathering epidemiological data and utilization records, while sensitive school records are obviously best left to the administrators and staff within the school.

The personal knowledge that members of the group may have of the student population is also invaluable for gaining insights into the realistic nature of the problem. Perceptual data in the form of anecdotal evidence supplied by members of the group who are intimately connected to the youth population can provide real-life stories and vignettes that may illustrate and uncover larger needs. However, anecdotal or perceptual evidence must be supported by other data sources to present a more accurate picture.

Additional data sources that support the group's initial observations and hypotheses might include county unemployment rates, social services to families of dependent children, census data related to children and youth under age 18, and dollar amounts spent on pupils per capita for the school district in comparison with neighboring areas—affluent areas in particular. Multiple data sources used in conjunction with each other elicit a fuller, more robust picture of the school community and the interrelated variables.

Case Example: Use of Qualitative and Quantitative Data

In a certain middle school, tardiness and absenteeism were attributed by members of the staff to specific needs related to lack of access to basic necessities such as child care, medical care, and clean clothes. As a guidance counselor reported in one school, "Alisha missed 20 days of school last year. In her case, some of those absences were a result of the family's lack of medical care. For example, one night her younger brother had to go the emergency room because he had developed a persistent cough that was later diagnosed as bronchitis. The family used the emergency room because they had no medical coverage. That was on Tuesday night, when the family normally went to the laundromat. The next day, Alisha had no clean clothes to wear to school so she stayed home. On many occasions she has to walk her younger siblings to school. Their school starts an hour later than the middle school so she is frequently late."

The group then supported these assumptions by looking at the community and school data related to poverty and economic need. Tardy and absentee records were disaggregated according to race, ethnicity, and socioeconomic status. Free and reduced lunch data indicated high levels of poverty within the school. The group also looked at the high utilization rates at the hospital emergency room by uninsured families as another indicator.

Conducting Surveys and Forums

The invaluable perspectives of the main constituents of the school community, namely students and their families, are often not captured through formal data sources. Listening to these vital voices is a key to crafting successful interventions. There is no substitute for field data. It is recommended that the team conduct its own data-retrieval process through surveys, formal and informal student and parent forums, surveys posted on the school web site or in the local newspaper, or interviews conducted with randomly selected students and parents.

Local colleges and universities can often be helpful by supplying student interns who may be willing to help in this process. Community partners such as mental health agencies and youth service organizations can also be helpful in data gathering. Figure 5.5 (page 131) shows a sample student survey, and Figure 5.6 (page 139) shows a sample parent survey.

Figure 5.5. Student Survey

Element 1: Safety of the Physical Plant					
In terms of school safety, this school has:	**No**	**Not really**	**Some**	**Mostly**	**Yes**
	1	**2**	**3**	**4**	**5**
1. Clean walls inside and out with no graffiti.					
2. Clean hallways and classrooms with no garbage.					
3. Well-lit hallways, bathrooms, and classrooms.					
4. Wide hallways and stairs with room to pass comfortably.					
5. Offices located near the main entrance.					
6. Bathrooms located near main traffic area, not in isolated locations.					
7. Classrooms clustered by grade level.					
8. Space for all students; not overcrowded.					
9. Security in the form of cameras, alarms, or some type of hall monitor or security guard.					
10. Close monitoring of any isolated areas inside and outside.					
11. Clean air.					
12. Safety plan communicated to students about what to do in cases of emergency.					
Comment:					

Figure 5.5. Student Survey (continues)

Element 2: Shared Leadership Practices					
The principal of this school:	**Not at all**	**Once in awhile**	**Some-times**	**A lot**	**All the time**
	1	**2**	**3**	**4**	**5**
1. Invites students to participate in decision-making committees, such as the school safety team, etc.					
2. Communicates directly with students on a regular basis.					
3. Uses newsletters, web sites, and other ways to regularly communicate with students.					
4. Communicates a belief that all students can achieve excellence.					
5. Communicates a clear vision for the school community.					
Comments:					

Element 3: Structured Personalized Learning Communities					
In this school:	Never	Once in awhile	Some-times	A lot	Always
	1	2	3	4	5
1. We are divided into teams.					
2. I know the other students in my grade.					
3. Teachers give me individual attention.					
4. I know the other students in the school.					
5. My teachers offer me help in dealing with personal problems if I need it.					
6. I have had the same teacher for two grades in a row.					
7. I have an adult advisor in the school with whom I meet regularly.					
8. My adult advisor knows what is going on with me in school, with family, and in other parts of my life.					
9. I have a mentor in the school or community.					
10. There are programs to help you when you are first entering this school: a buddy, an orientation, a welcome center, etc.					
11. I am part of an afterschool program.					
12. I have spoken to the social worker or student assistance counselor.					
Comments:					

Figure 5.5. Student Survey (continues)

Element 4: Student-Centered Learning Practices					
In this school:	Never	Once in awhile	Some-times	A lot	Always
	1	2	3	4	5
1. I have opportunities to make my own learning goals.					
2. My teachers have taught me how to do self-assessments, like giving myself a grade for my homework or project.					
3. My teachers have taught me how to do peer assessments and evaluations, like giving them a grade on a joint project.					
4. I have opportunities to work in teams with other students in the class.					
5. I have opportunities to work in teams with other students on special projects.					
6. I have opportunities to work within small groups with students who are different from me.					
7. I learn skills like how to get along with other people, how to work in teams, etc.					
8. I have opportunities to participate in community service or service learning programs.					
9. My teachers give me immediate personal feedback on how I did on my tests, class assignments, and homework.					
10. Teachers give me recognition for good work.					
11. Teachers are fair to everyone, regardless of their race, ethnicity, gender or social class.					
Comments:					

Element 5: Caring Relationships and Sense of Community					
In this school:	**Never**	**Once in awhile**	**Some-times**	**A lot**	**Always**
	1	**2**	**3**	**4**	**5**
1. Teachers and other adults care about me.					
2. Teachers provide extra help if I need it.					
3. Teachers listen to me.					
4. Teachers praise me.					
5. I have opportunities to make decisions about what happens in the classroom and in the school.					
6. I know what my teachers expect from me.					
7. I want to do well in school and get good grades.					
8. I spend enough time studying and doing home-work and class work to get good grades.					
9. Doing well in school is helpful later on in life.					
10. I agree with the goals of this school.					
11. I care about what my teachers think about me.					
12. I feel part of this school.					
13. I participate in many school activities.					
14. I have a good relationship with most of my teachers.					
15. When the work is more difficult, I work harder rather than just give up.					
16. I have a lot of friends at school.					
17. I have kids I like in my classes.					
18. I feel accepted and like I belong in this school.					
19. I have an adult who regularly talks to me about what is going on for me with school.					

Figure 5.5. Student Survey (continues)

Element 6: Schoolwide Positive Discipline and Self-Management Practices					
In this school:	Never	Once in awhile	Some-times	A lot	Always
	1	2	3	4	5
1. I learn skills for making healthy decisions, how to solve problems without fighting, and getting along with different types of people.					
2. I regularly learn these social skills in all our core classes.					
3. I learn positive behaviors for class, lunch-time, hallways, recess, ans before and after school.					
4. I am asked to give my ideas about class and school rules.					
5. I have opportunities to participate in class meetings and speak about my opinions and ideas.					
6. Teachers and other staff show me respect and treat me politely without yelling or ordering me around.					
7. I regularly receive recognition for positive behavior.					
8. I know the school rules.					
9. The school enforces discipline fairly for all students.					
10. The school lets my family know about my accomplishments in school.					
11. I receive public recognition for my schoolwork, artwork, or positive behavior on a regular basis.					
12. Getting recognition makes me feel good about myself and my accomplishments.					
Comments:					

Element 7: Active Staff, Student, Family, and Community Involvement					
In this school, students are	**Never**	**Once in awhile**	**Some-times**	**A lot**	**Always**
	1	**2**	**3**	**4**	**5**
1. Regularly asked their opinions and thoughts about how the school runs.					
2. Asked to help develop the Codes of Conduct, Safety Plan, and other policies.					
3. Given choices about their learning goals and the ways they can best learn.					
4. Involved in deciding how the class rules for how students behave.					
5. Treated respectfully by being expected to manage their own behavior.					
6. Supported by their family to do well in school.					
7. Supported by the school in helping their family understand how they are doing in school.					
Comments:					

Figure 5.5. Student Survey (continues)

Student Demographic Data

Please fill in the circles or blanks for the five questions listed below:

1. I am:
   (Fill in any or all circles that apply.)
   ❍ African American
   ❍ American Indian (Native American)
   ❍ Asian
   ❍ Biracial
   ❍ Caucasian (White)
   ❍ Hispanic (Latino)
   ❍ Middle Eastern
   ❍ Other: ____________________

2. I am in grade _____

3. I came to this school in grade _____

4. I am:
   ❍ Male
   ❍ Female

5. I participate in or have participated in (in the past two years):
   (Fill in any or all circles that apply.)
   ❍ Sports
   ❍ Music, band, orchestra
   ❍ Peer leadership
   ❍ School club
   ❍ Community activity
   ❍ Not involved in any activity

Figure 5.6. Parent Survey

Element 1: Safety of the Physical Plant					
In terms of the school safety plan:	**No**	**Not really**	**Some**	**Mostly**	**Yes**
	1	**2**	**3**	**4**	**5**
1. Parents are involved in the development.					
2. It is communicated and accessible to parents.					
Comments:					

Element 2: Shared Leadership Practices					
The principal of this school:	**Not at all**	**Once in awhile**	**Some-times**	**A lot**	**All the time**
	1	**2**	**3**	**4**	**5**
1. Invites parents to participate in decision-making committees such as the school safety team.					
2. Regularly communicates directly with parents.					
3. Uses newsletters, web sites, and other ways to regularly communicate with families.					
Comments:					

Figure 5.6. Parent Survey (continues)

Element 3: Structured Personalized Learning Community					
In this school:	**Never**	**Seldom**	**Some-times**	**A lot**	**Always**
	1	**2**	**3**	**4**	**5**
1. I am invited to become involved in services and programs within the school.					
2. I have spoken to the guidance counselor or social worker.					
3. I feel comfortable asking staff for help with referrals to community services.					
4. There is an adult who regularly talks to my child about what is going on with school and other issues.					
5. Teachers encourage my child to do well in school.					
6. I was invited to an orientation for new students just entering the school.					
7. My child has an older student or adult who serves as a mentor or buddy.					
If this school has an afterschool program:					
8. I have been notified and invited to have my child participate in the afterschool program.					
9. I have been invited to participate as a parent.					
Comments:					

Element 4: Student-Centered Learning Practices					
In this school:	Never	Seldom	Some-times	A lot	Always
	1	2	3	4	5
1. My child has opportunities to participate in community service programs.					
2. My child has opportunities to work in teams with other students on special projects.					
3. There is an adult who regularly talks to my child about what is going on in school.					
4. My child has a student or adult mentor.					
5. My child is encouraged to do well in school by his/her teachers.					
6. Staff treat all families in a fair and equal way.					
7. Staff treat me in a positive and respectful way.					
8. I am invited to attend school presentations.					
9. I am welcome at my child's school.					
10. Staff try to schedule meetings at times convenient for me and other parents.					
11. Staff give me a choice of meeting times instead of just giving me one time.					
12. Staff talk about the strengths of my child instead of just problems.					
13. Staff make it easy to communicate with them through letter, notes, phone, e-mail, etc.					
Comments:					

Figure 5.6. Parent Survey (continues)

Element 5: Caring Relationship and Sense of Community					
In this school:	**Not at all**	**Once in awhile**	**Some times**	**A lot**	**All the time**
	1	**2**	**3**	**4**	**5**
1. Staff demonstrate the ability to relate to different types of families.					
2. Staff treat all families in a fair and equal way.					
3. Staff treat me in a positive and respectful way.					
4. I am invited to attend school presentations.					
5. I am welcome at my child's school.					
6. Staff try to schedule meetings at times convenient for me and other parents.					
7. Staff give me a choice of meeting times instead of just giving me one time.					
8. Staff talk about the strengths of my child instead of just problems.					
9. Staff make it easy to communicate with them through letter, notes, phone, e-mail, etc.					
Comments:					

Element 6: Schoolwide Positive Discipline and Self-Management Practices					
This school:	**Never**	**Seldom**	**Some-times**	**A lot**	**Always**
	1	**2**	**3**	**4**	**5**
1. Frequently displays student work in the school and community.					
2. Frequently recognizes students and notifies parents of the recognition.					
3. Regularly notifies me of my child's achievements.					
Comments:					

Element 7: Active Family Involvement					
In this school, as a parent I am:	**Never**	**Seldom**	**Some-times**	**A lot**	**Always**
	1	**2**	**3**	**4**	**5**
1. Regularly asked my opinions and thoughts about how the school runs.					
2. Asked to help develop the Codes of Conduct, Safety Plan, and other policies.					
3. Supported by the school in understanding how my child is doing in school.					
4. Involved in developing and implementing parent-involvement strategies.					
5. Asked about how I think the school can best involve parents.					
6. Included in team training for data analysis, etc. when serving on committees.					
Comments:					

Figure 5.6. Parent Survey (continues)

Family Demographic Data

Please fill in the circles or blanks for the four questions listed below:

1. I am:
   (Fill in any or all the circles that apply.)
   - ❍ African American
   - ❍ American Indian (Native American)
   - ❍ Asian
   - ❍ Biracial
   - ❍ Caucasian (White)
   - ❍ Hispanic (Latino)
   - ❍ Middle Eastern
   - ❍ Other: ____________________

2. I am:
   - ❍ Male
   - ❍ Female

3. The primary language spoken in my home is: _________________

4. I have completed my education:
   (Fill in any or all the circles that apply.)
   - ❍ 9th grade or less
   - ❍ GED
   - ❍ High school diploma
   - ❍ Vocational training
   - ❍ Associate degree
   - ❍ Some college
   - ❍ College degree
   - ❍ Master's degree
   - ❍ Doctorate

Community Resource Mapping

An important source of data that is often overlooked in school improvement efforts has to do with the assets and resources available to students and their parents in the community. This is particularly valuable when developing supportive learning environments. Student learning is enhanced through the types of mentoring and service learning programs often found in community-based agencies. Schools have increasingly begun to initiate these types of programs in partnership with community organizations. (Refer to Chapter 3 for a thorough discussion of these strategies.) See Figure 5.7 (page 146) for a worksheet for community resource mapping.

Figure 5.7. Community Resource Mapping

Mark the names of the various organizations and resources within your community on the map. These organizations might include recreational programs, youth programs like the YMCA, faith-based youth and family programs, public libraries, hospitals and public medical and mental health services, senior citizens' services, low-income and homeless housing programs, child care service providers, local food pantries, transportation systems within the community, higher education, businesses, and local law enforcement.

Community organizations and agencies are vitally important for providing families with needed resources such as food, housing, medical care, mental health services, and child care. Often, as illustrated by the guidance counselor's story of Alisha, a student's attendance and achievement can be greatly affected by the family's lack of resources to basic necessities. Often, school social workers and guidance counselors, acting in concert with community agencies, can provide valuable assistance and restore equilibrium to a family that is experiencing major stress and difficulty in dealing with basic survival needs.

School-community collaborations are enhanced through intentional partnerships with agencies within the community. Often, the process of community resource mapping initiates linkages between the school and the community in developing additional supports or strengthening existing supports for students and their families. Some schools have evolved strategies of listing these services to families in the community in their school calendar, on their web sites, in the local newspaper, and on the local TV and radio stations. This enhances relations with the school and community and gives these media outlets an opportunity to perform a valuable community service by providing free public service announcements.

Phase Four: Uncover the Needs through Data

The team will use the guiding questions (see Figure 5.8, page 148) to focus the discussions using multiple data sources and will arrive more quickly at grounded conclusions about the nature of the problem areas and the reasons for their successes.

Figure 5.8. Guiding Questions

- What is our vision of a supportive learning environment? (Restate the vision.)
- What is going well in our schools? (Strengths-based assessment.)
- Who are the students and families that seem to be receiving the maximum benefit and support from our learning community? (Disaggregate by race, SES, gender, ability groupings, and age.)
- Why is this happening? (Generate hypothesis and causal analysis.)
- What questions do we need to ask? (Generate questions.)
- What evidence do we have to support our assumptions? (Generate data sources.)
- What additional sources of data do we need to look at?
- What is not going well in our schools? (Focus on areas for improvement.)
- Who are the students and families that seem to be receiving the least benefit and support from our learning community? (Disaggregate by race, SES, gender, ability groupings, and age.)
- Why is this happening? (Generate hypothesis and causal analysis.)
- What questions do we need to ask? (Generate questions.)
- What evidence do we have to support our assumptions? (Generate data sources.)
- What additional sources of data do we need to look at?
- What are the major areas of need?
- What are the top priorities?
- What evidence supports this?
- What research-based strategies are most effective at addressing these areas?

Examine Data from Multiple Perspectives

At this point, the team is ready to explore the data more fully. The team has been primed through the predata explorations and can now move to the actual data to support or refute their hunches and hypotheses. Use multiple data sources throughout the discussion. Look for patterns, trends, and gaps. Look at relationships and comparisons between data sets.

Specifically, look at grade level, incoming students, and outgoing students. Look at time factors such as time of day, month, and year. Look at family and community resources and assets in addition to school resources. Study the relationships and interrelationships for students and families (disaggregated by race, ethnicity, socioeconomic status, gender, ability groupings, age) between variables such as levels of achievement and participation in extracurricular or afterschool activities, parental involvement and student achievement, caring relationships between students and teachers, and decrease in student discipline referrals. We know from the research that these variables are interrelated. The team needs to examine these variables in their own school and community. (See Chapter 3 for a complete discussion on these variables and indicators of student learning and performance).

Team members use the same guiding questions discussed earlier in this chapter to explore what is going on in their school. They can begin to focus their discussions through the use of multiple data sources and arrive more quickly at grounded conclusions about the nature of the problem areas and the reasons for their successes.

Explore the Guiding Questions with Data

Use the guiding questions. The team needs to stay grounded in the data during this process and support any and all conclusions with evidence (refer to Figure 5.8, page 148).

What Are We Doing Currently That's Working?

Look at increases, decreases, or stability in student achievement over time. What about parent involvement? Even if only small minorities of parents are currently engaged in school, this should still be viewed as a starting point and account for at least some measure of school success. What are the activities and the level of student involvement in extracurricular activities? Where are there decreases in discipline referrals? These can be done as comparison measures across time or grade levels.

For Whom Is It Working?

This involves disaggregating key data that looks at student achievement, discipline referrals, truancy, dropout rates, and parent and student involvement to determine who is benefiting from current practices and who is not. Disaggregation refers to looking at students by grade, age, years in school, race, ethnicity, socioeconomic status, gender, learning disabilities, English language learners, and other measures that the team may decide are relevant.

What's Not Working? For Whom Is It Not Working?

Some of these questions will be answered through the comparison of disaggregated data for student and family groupings. They are also answered in part through contrasting what is working for whom and examining who is left out of that equation. For example, if scores are going up for middle-class white students and middle-class students of color, the team needs to explore, and support with evidence, the logical conclusion that scores are remaining low for poor white students and poor students of color. Further explorations might also uncover that English language learners and special education students are part of the group for whom interventions are not working.

In addition, a careful assessment of timelines involving new interventions compared with any increases or decreases in student measures should yield valuable information about whether some practices are not yielding expected results within a realistic timeframe. In other words, have referrals increased or decreased within the first six months since implementing a new discipline policy? Do these results conform to our projections and expectations? What is the effect of the new discipline policy on the number of incidents of violent and disruptive behaviors? When results are disaggregated, which student populations account for the greatest and the fewest number of incidents?

What Do We Need to Do More of or Strengthen? What Do We Need to Do Less of or Eliminate?

The needs that get uncovered in this process might point to assets as well as areas for improvement. Assets might include things that are working well, such as existing resources, strategies, and practices. However, an analysis might find that these assets need to be strengthened to reach all students, or additional work must be done to sustain them and embed them in the system. Areas for improvement can highlight gaps in services to students and families. They can pinpoint current practices, procedures, and policies that may be detrimental to some students and families, and can also undermine staff morale. These areas will be the most challenging to ascertain, of course, because they involve the most substantial implications for change within the system.

Exercise: Case Scenario—Needs Assessment

Read the following case scenario and have the team identify key strengths and key areas of need based on the data:

Hillside High School has conducted a data study using multiple tools. Areas of strength include a slight increase in student achievement in 10th grade with a small though steady incremental increase in 11th and 12th grade. An overall student dropout rate for the school has declined slightly in the past three years.

The school reports significant problems, however, many of which require immediate attention. School records show an alarming trend in decreased achievement on test scores and exams, and increased truancy, discipline referrals, and dropouts over the past year. Disaggregated data show a consistent pattern. Poor students, students of color, special education students, and recent immigrants who are English language learners are overrepresented in the low achievement and high rates of dropouts, truancy, and discipline referrals. A surprising finding for the team was that the 9th graders have the highest rates of dropouts, as well as the lowest achievement scores and the highest discipline referrals in the school.

Community resource mapping uncovered very few youth-oriented programs for middle school and high school students. The local chapter of the YMCA has an afterschool program for grades 5–9. On closer examination, it was revealed that there is a significant drop-off in service utilization for students after grade 6. An area church sponsors a youth club that involves youth aged 12–18. A small but dedicated group of parents are involved in the PTA and sponsor occasional special assemblies for students.

Little is known about services used by families. These records are difficult to obtain because there are very few joint community-school partnerships. In addition, relations with the community have been somewhat contentious, as a result of the school's poor performance and the perception in the community that the school is a dangerous place. This has been fueled in part by a recent stabbing, which was widely reported by the local papers.

Student surveys uncovered an interesting discrepancy in the measures of caring relationships, sense of community bonding and school connectedness: The school scored low on these measures in all grades. However, the lowest ratings came from the majority of 9th graders, as compared with slightly higher scores by the 10th, 11th, and 12th graders. Demographic data revealed that the lowest scores came from students of color, poor students, and special education students.

Parent surveys uncovered several patterns; on the measure of feeling "supported by the school in understanding how my child is doing in school," parents of 10 to 12th graders were more likely to report that they felt supported than parents of 9th graders. Further disaggregation of available demographic data revealed that the majority of respondents were white families. Lower rates of survey completion by parents of students of color were noted by the team. Additional measures were used to engage this population, including community forums and bilingual interpreters. These measures yielded greater numbers of parents who completed the survey. Overall, the surveys reported slightly higher scores for Latino families than for African American families, but lower than for white families on the same measure of feeling "supported by the school in understanding how my child is doing in school."

Exercise: Case Scenario—Team Findings

- Compare your team's findings with the Hillside High School Team's findings for areas of strength and areas of need.
- Some success in raising student achievement and lowering dropout rates in grades 10–12. The team thought it might be advisable to explore if any new programs or practices had been introduced recently at these grade levels that might account for the modest success.
- Low achievement scores of 9th graders, particularly among poor students, students of color, special education students, and recent immigrants who were English language learners. The team agreed that this area needed to be examined and strategies developed to address this achievement gap.
- Poor communication with parents, particularly parents of 9th graders, poor parents, and parents of color. The team saw this as a need to increase support for 9th graders and their parents in orienting them to school and a need for greater communication with all parents, particularly poor parents and parents of color.
- Some parent involvement. The team had some recent success in engaging parents in the needs-assessment process. They saw this as a good start and felt that it indicated a need that parents were expressing to be more actively engaged by the school in developing strategies to enhance the learning environment. The active members of the PTA were also seen as an asset that could be strengthened by inclusion of more and different types of parents.
- High rates of discipline referrals for 9th graders, particularly among poor students, students of color, special education students, and recent immigrants who were English language learners. The team saw this as a clear need to examine and revamp discipline policies and practices.
- Student perceptions of a lack of caring relationships, sense of community bonding, and school connectedness, particularly among 9th graders, students of color, poor students, and special education students. The team saw this as a need to increase student engagement in school through developing strategies and structures to personalize the learning environment.
- High truancy and dropout rates, particularly among the 9th graders, poor students, students of color, special education students, and recent immigrants who were English language learners at all grade levels. The team identified this as a need to learn more about students' reasons for being truant and/or dropping out and what they would like in the school.
- Few youth resources in the community. The team saw this as an urgent need to create youth-oriented services within the school and partner with the community to develop more youth programming. They also wanted to find out from students which services they wanted and why the YMCA afterschool program was not being used by 7th–9th graders.
- Poor school-community relations. The team felt that this was related to the other factors of parent and community involvement. They identified this as a need for increased communication and involvement with the community.

6

Putting the Plan Together: Who's on First?

I for one believe that if you give people a thorough understanding of what confronts them and the basic causes that produce it, they'll create their own program, and when the people create a program, you get action.

Malcolm X

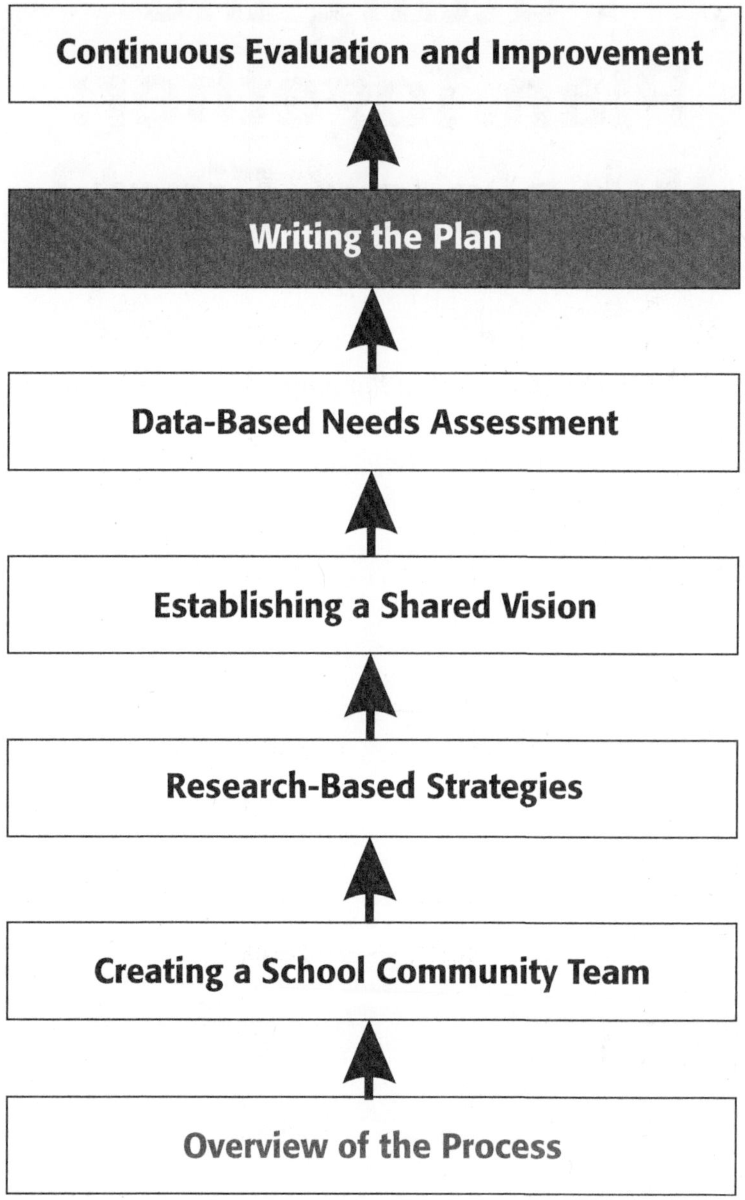
Continuous Evaluation and Improvement
Writing the Plan
Data-Based Needs Assessment
Establishing a Shared Vision
Research-Based Strategies
Creating a School Community Team
Overview of the Process

Writing a Workable Plan

Writing a workable plan allows the team to use these tools to answer the following questions:

- What have we determined are our needs in order of priority?
  Use Figure 6.1 (page 158): Prioritizing Needs.
- Which research-based strategies will we use to address these needs?
  Use Figure 6.2 (page 161): Strategy Selection: Matching Needs to Research-Based Strategies
- How will we prioritize our strategies?
  Use Figure 6.3 (page 167): Prioritizing Strategies: Checklist
- How will we sequence the implementation of our strategies?
  Use Figure 6.4 (page 169): Prioritizing Strategies: Sequence of Implementation
- How will we map our strategies to create cohesiveness and consistency?
  Use Figure 6.5 (page 172): Strategy Map
- What outcomes do we hope to achieve?
- What outputs do we hope to achieve?
- Which indicators will we use to let us know we've been successful?
- Which sources of data or information will we gather to show evidence of success?
- What action steps will we take in implementing our strategy?
- Who will do what?
- Within what time frames?
  Use Figure 6.6 (page 181): Action Plan Template

Prioritizing Needs

The group must distinguish between those activities that are urgent and important and those that are important but not urgent. Then it must distinguish immediate from longer-term strategies (see Figure 6.1, page 158).

Figure 6.1. Prioritizing Needs

Step 1: Determine whether need is urgent and important or important but not urgent. Write in the box.

Step 2: Determine whether need is immediate or longer term. Write in the box.

1. Select box	*Urgent and Important	*Important but Not Urgent
2. Select box	**Immediate**	**Longer Term**

*(*Adapted from Stephen Covey's Time Management Matrix)*

At this point in the process, the team has uncovered major needs by looking at the data and connecting the needs to the overall improvement and strategic goals of the school. Next, it must develop a manageable plan that is coherent and integrated with the school improvement plans.

A team can easily become overwhelmed by trying to accomplish everything at once. The group must distinguish between urgent and important needs and between immediate and longer-term strategies. These distinctions will help create a logical sequence for implementation. Prioritizing needs and strategies will go a long way toward developing a successful plan.

The needs uncovered by the team cannot all be elevated to the level of extreme urgency. This is a sure fire recipe for burnout. As Stephen Covey states: "The two factors that define an activity are *urgent* and *important. Urgent* means it requires immediate attention. *Importance,* on the other hand, has to do with results. If something is important, it contributes to your mission, your values, your high priority goals" (1989, p. 150–151). The team must differentiate between those activities that are urgent and important and those that are important but not urgent. Urgent and important needs should be your top priority. They generally concern immediate safety issues that must be attended to before other interventions can be attempted. Important but not urgent issues should be part of a longer-term intervention that might require more time to plan and implement. Most of what the team will uncover falls into this category. Scaffold these interventions by sequencing them in an order that logically builds one upon the other to create sustainable changes in the entire system.

In dealing with students and the conditions that affect learning, everything is important, but not necessarily urgent. If there isn't a day that goes by without a fight breaking out among the 9th grade students, the situation is urgent and important. If the school got a grant to create a parent center and no parents show up, that is important but not urgent. Both will affect student learning. One is of immediate concern because it can escalate into a crisis. One is part of longer-term planning because it is important, but does not qualify as a crisis or a situation that poses an imminent threat. Often the greatest and most sustainable changes come from addressing the important but nonurgent needs.

Underlying issues can be the same in both situations (for example, as a lack of parent involvement, a lack of multicultural competence, or a lack of connection between adults and students). Strategies that address these important but not urgent needs are usually interconnected and complementary, such as training the staff in multicultural competence to become more effective at engaging parents and students in the education process, or creating a transition or advisory program that engages students and families in a more personal way with school staff.

Matching Needs to Research Based Strategies

The team now matches the needs to corresponding research-based practices and structures that provide the greatest likelihood of improving the learning environment (see Figure 6.2, page 161). After key areas of focus have been identified and supported by evidence, they need to be correlated with research-based strategies and promising practices. This allows the team to take advantage of the most accurate and rigorous work in the field of developing supportive learning environments without having to become research scientists or go through the costly (and probably impractical) process of evaluating existing programs for proven effectiveness. (See Chapter 3 for a detailed description of research-based strategies in developing supportive learning environments.)

Figure 6.2. Strategy Selection: Matching Needs to Research-Based Strategies

#	Area of Need	Research-Based Strategy
1		
2		
3		
4		

Figure 6.2. (Continues)

<table>
<tr><th colspan="3">Exercise: Case Scenario: Matching Needs to Research-Based Strategies</th></tr>
<tr><td colspan="3">Compare your team's strategy selections to that of Hillside High School.</td></tr>
<tr><th>#</th><th>Area of Need: Immediate</th><th>Research-Based Strategy</th></tr>
<tr><td>1</td><td>9th grade student perceptions of a lack of caring relationships, sense of community bonding and school connectedness—especially among poor students, students of color, special education students, and recent immigrants who were English language learners

Strategies may also address:
▪ High truancy rates
▪ High dropout rates
▪ Poor communication with parents of 9th graders</td><td>Transition programs
Increase student achievement, enhance sense of community, and reduce dropouts
▪ Provide all 8th grade students and parents with information about the high school through a series of orientation sessions
▪ Bring together staff from the two schools to learn about and provide linkages between the schools and one another's programs.
▪ Provide students and parents with Student and Parent Buddies during the first year in school (may hold for a later intervention)
Advisory programs
Advisory groups function as support systems for 9th graders.

Every student is assigned to one adult.
▪ Advisors have daily interactions with students.
▪ Staff receives training on role of advisor.
▪ Advisors act as liaisons between teachers and students and are the maintain contact with parents about student progress in all subjects.</td></tr>
</table>

#	Area of Need: Longer Term	Research-Based Strategy
2	High rates of discipline referrals for 9th graders ▪ Disproportionate representation of poor students, students of color, special education students, and recent immigrants who are English language learners in issues of truancy, dropping out	**Consistent and fair enforcement of rules** Creates active student involvement and buy-in. ▪ Input is actively solicited and incorporated into schoolwide rule making from all constituent groups, including students, parents, and faculty. ▪ School rules are established and communicated. **Equitable discipline policy** Ensures equal treatment for all. ▪ Monitor suspensions, expulsions, and alternative placements to avoid disproportionate representation of minorities in suspensions, expulsions, and discipline referrals. **Daily reinforcement of decision making and social skills** Reduces risk behavior. ▪ Self-management practices are actively employed in the school and classroom ▪ Skill practice is incorporated into daily activities (may hold for a later intervention).
3	Disproportionate representation among poor students, students of color, special education students and recent immigrants who are English language learners in issues of truancy, dropping out, discipline referrals, and low academic achievement	**Multicultural competence training** Improves relationships and diversity skills. ▪ Staff and students receive training in multicultural competence. ▪ Staff exhibit high expectations for all students and families. ▪ Staff exhibit equitable interactions with all students and families. ▪ Students learn how to interact fairly and equitably with others of different race, ethnicity, gender.

#	Area of Need: Longer Term	Research-Based Strategy
	(#3 continues)	**Student-centered instruction and assessment practices are employed** Improves relationships between students and teachers and between students and students. ▪ Teachers are trained in student-centered learning techniques. ▪ Students are encouraged to control their own learning through contracting around setting goals, subgoals, and corresponding grades. ▪ Students are given opportunities for self-assessment and student-led peer feedback. ▪ Teachers engage in contracting with students around personalized learning and instructional goals.
4	Some success in engaging parents in the needs assessment process	**Parents are actively involved in developing and implementing parent involvement strategies** Increases parent involvement that is positively correlated with student achievement. ▪ School includes parents as partners in developing strategies for parents. ▪ Parents are instrumental in determining how to effectively uncover and meet parent needs. ▪ Parents are utilized as resources in the delivery of parent services. **Parents are aware of their child's progress in school** ▪ School actively informs parents of child's progress. ▪ School has a variety of communication methods for reaching parents, including letters, phone, e-mail, and media outlets

A careful review of the strategies described in Figure 3.2 (page 66), Indicators of Success, will provide the team with an understanding of the goals and parameters of the specified interventions. The team must be clear on what these interventions can accomplish, what the goals are for implementing them, how the interventions can be tailored to meet specific needs, and what the scope of the intervention is in terms of who may be affected in the broadest sense. For example, an advisory program can contain elements that benefit students directly, benefit the staff that engage in closer relationships with students and each other, and benefit parents who are part of an enlarged communication process. Additionally, strategies such as an advisory program can be tailored to include components of mentoring, service learning, class and group discussions, and student-led activities.

The Dynamic Process of Change

This is a dynamic process in that the team will need to discuss and evaluate which areas of need can best be addressed by which research-based strategies. There is no set equation such as x need = x strategy. Rather than a direct one-to-one correlation between problem and solution, the team needs to think more holistically and understand that one or more interventions can be used in concert with each other and that the series of interventions can in turn address more than one area of need.

As discussed with advisory programs, this strategy can be used to address the need for increased sense of community, create improved relations between students and teachers, strengthen a continuum of supports in the school, and enhance parent involvement and communication. The team needs to think creatively—to envision the strategy and how it can be shaped to meet multiple needs.

Manageable Strategies

Like focusing on areas for improvement, strategy selection should be kept to a manageable level so that the team has a reasonable chance of implementing strategies successfully. Remember that these strategies and interventions act as scaffolds for future planning and implementation. As with the prior phase of prioritization, strategies should be limited to ensure greater success in implementation. Recommendations are to limit the number of attempted interventions to no more than two or three, matching them up with the selected areas of need.

A few well-designed and carefully implemented strategies can have a greater impact than a plethora of programs thrown at the problem. Thoughtful sequencing and scaffolding of the interventions can lead to a solid foundation that will be embedded in the structure and sustainable over time. The team will need to continuously revisit the strategy implementation and assess the success. Adjustments to the process can be made to refine it, to improve it, or to expand it. In this way, scaffolding and sequencing interventions can strengthen successful strategies and build continuous improvement across the system.

Prioritizing Strategies

The key to being able to address both short- and longer-term planning needs is to develop a realistic set of criteria that can be used to order the implementation of strategies. Sequence your strategies using criteria included in the checklist shown in Figure 6.3 or develop criteria decided upon by the team. Look at each strategy and make decisions about which one might be least complex to implement; most accessible in terms of the available human and fiscal resources; most doable given the current capacity in terms of time, energy, and competing initiatives of the school; most foundational to other strategies; or most easily accepted by school community. Use this checklist to decide which strategies are the most easily implemented first, second, and third.

Figure 6.3. Prioritizing Strategies: Checklist

Strategy	Trained staff are available	Access to training resources	Likelihood of acceptance in school	Fiscal resources are available	Does not compete for staff time with other initiatives	Builds foundation for other strategies

The Sequence of Change Efforts

Understanding the sequence of change efforts is an important aspect of building systemic change (see Figure 6.4, page 169). The deeper systemic changes are often referred to as *second order changes* and can require greater buy-in and collaboration from the school community and more time to implement than first order changes (Waters, Marzano, & McNulty, 2003). The team needs to look critically at the current climate and assess the readiness and willingness of the school community to embark on change. Sometimes, a short-term intervention that yields signs of immediate success can be a powerful motivator in attempting a longer term, more complex strategy.

Figure 6.4. Prioritizing Strategies: Sequence of Implementation

Sequence your strategies in order of implementation.

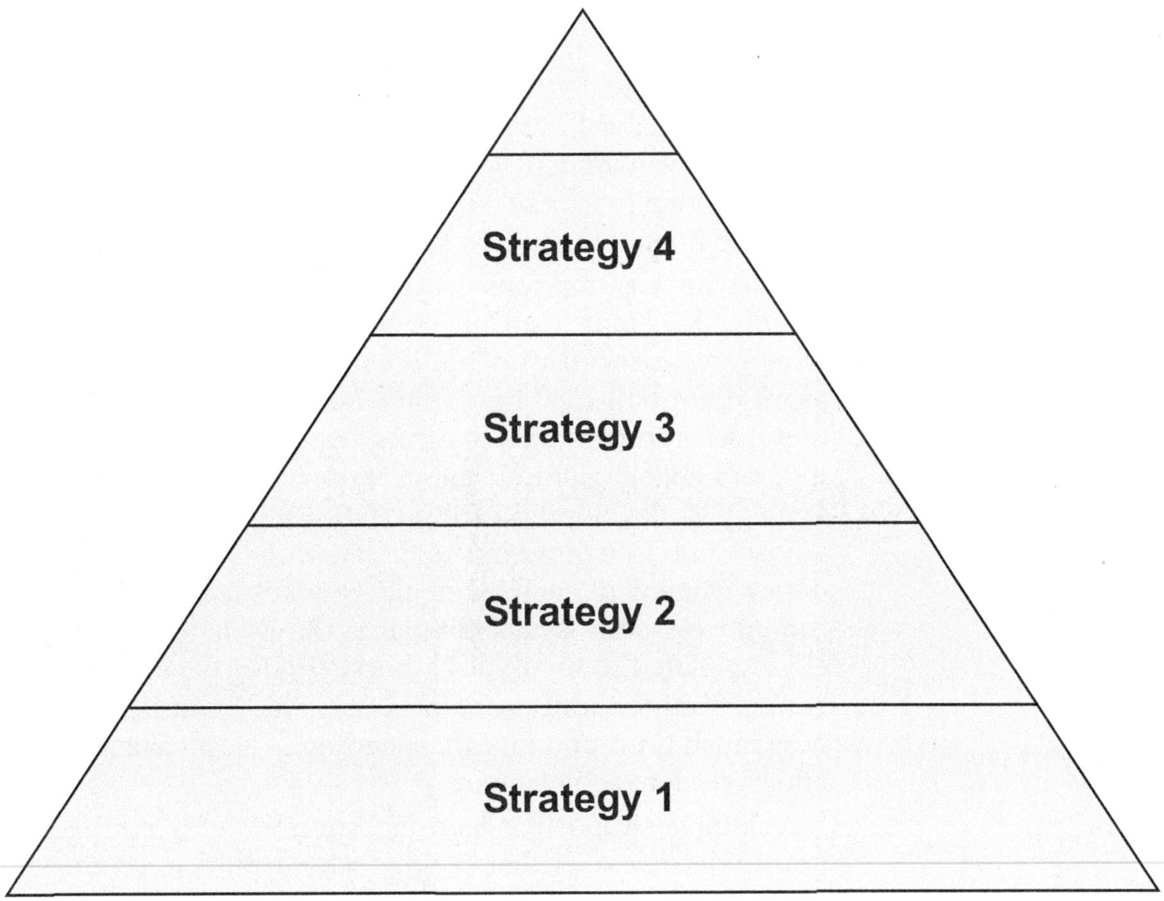

When change efforts are properly designed and sequenced, the important but nonurgent needs are often ameliorated and even resolved through the interventions that happen in the shorter term. Building the structures of supportive learning environments can address both the urgent and the important needs and minimize the crises. This frees up valuable energy in the system to continue to focus on improvement.

The team needs to address the urgent needs and as many of the important needs as is feasible. The recommendation is to limit the number of needs that the team will address to a manageable level, which depends on the composition of the team and the available human and fiscal resources to deal with the areas for improvement. Generally, it as advisable to start with no more than five or six areas of focus and then narrow them down to no more than two to three strategies.

Underlying assumptions about the order of change must be examined so that team members can become clearer about which areas of need are actually symptoms of other needs. For example, at Hillside High, truancy is most likely a symptom of the self-reported lack of caring relationships, school bonding, and engagement on the part of students. Therefore, the strategy of developing caring relationships through student advisor/advisee programs or developing tools for active student engagement such as regular student-led class meetings can address both issues. Similarly, the issue of discipline is closely related to the issues around truancy, so similar interventions might address both issues. And both issues affect how much time students are spending in class, which in turn affects student achievement.

Developing supportive learning environments addresses a multitude of issues that plague schools and interfere with learning, from truancy to dropouts, from fights to drugs and pregnancy. Action planning and careful strategy selection can remove these barriers to learning and build the foundation for a learning environment in which students are truly free to learn. Thoughtful sequencing of the interventions can be time- and energy-efficient and can yield successful results for students. This in turn builds confidence in the school to attempt broader and more extensive interventions that get to the heart of the underlying structure and fundamentally change the way in which the school does business.

Keeping the Big Picture in Mind: The Strategy Map

It is important to have a graphic way to envision how various strategies and interventions work together to create a whole. The team needs to map out the strategies to ensure that these strategies interact with each other to support a cohesive and coherent system of teaching and learning for the entire school.

The team can begin by using the Strategy Map (see Figure 6.5, page 172). This can also be a useful tool for explaining the process to staff, parents, students and community members and act as a graphic organizer for the planning team.

Figure 6.5. Strategy Map

Case Study:
Mapping Research-Based Strategies

Remember the team from Hillside High School who we encountered in Chapter 5? See if you can map their strategies (see Figures 5.6, page 139 and 5.8, page 148).

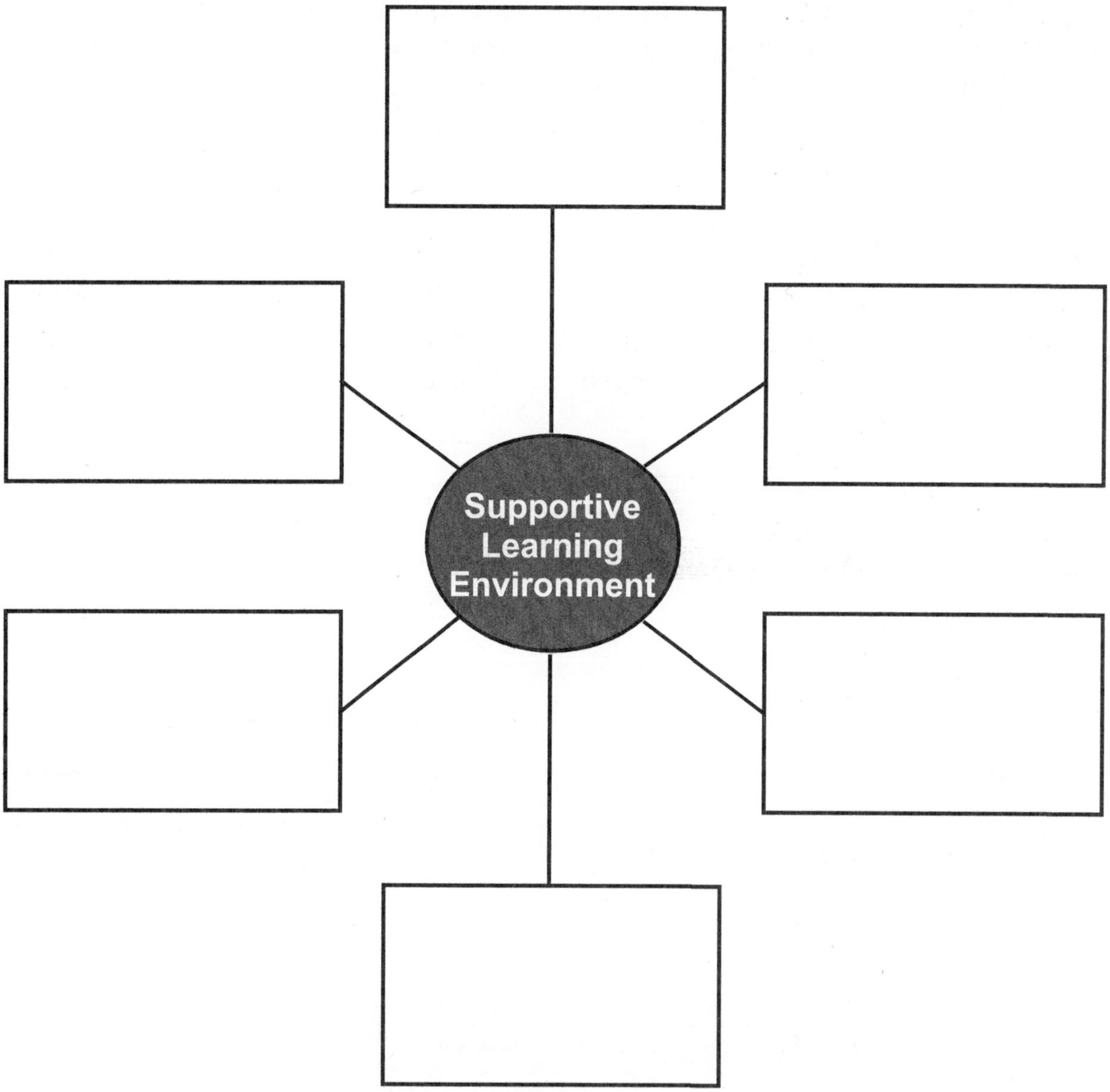

Figure 6.5. Strategy Map Worksheet

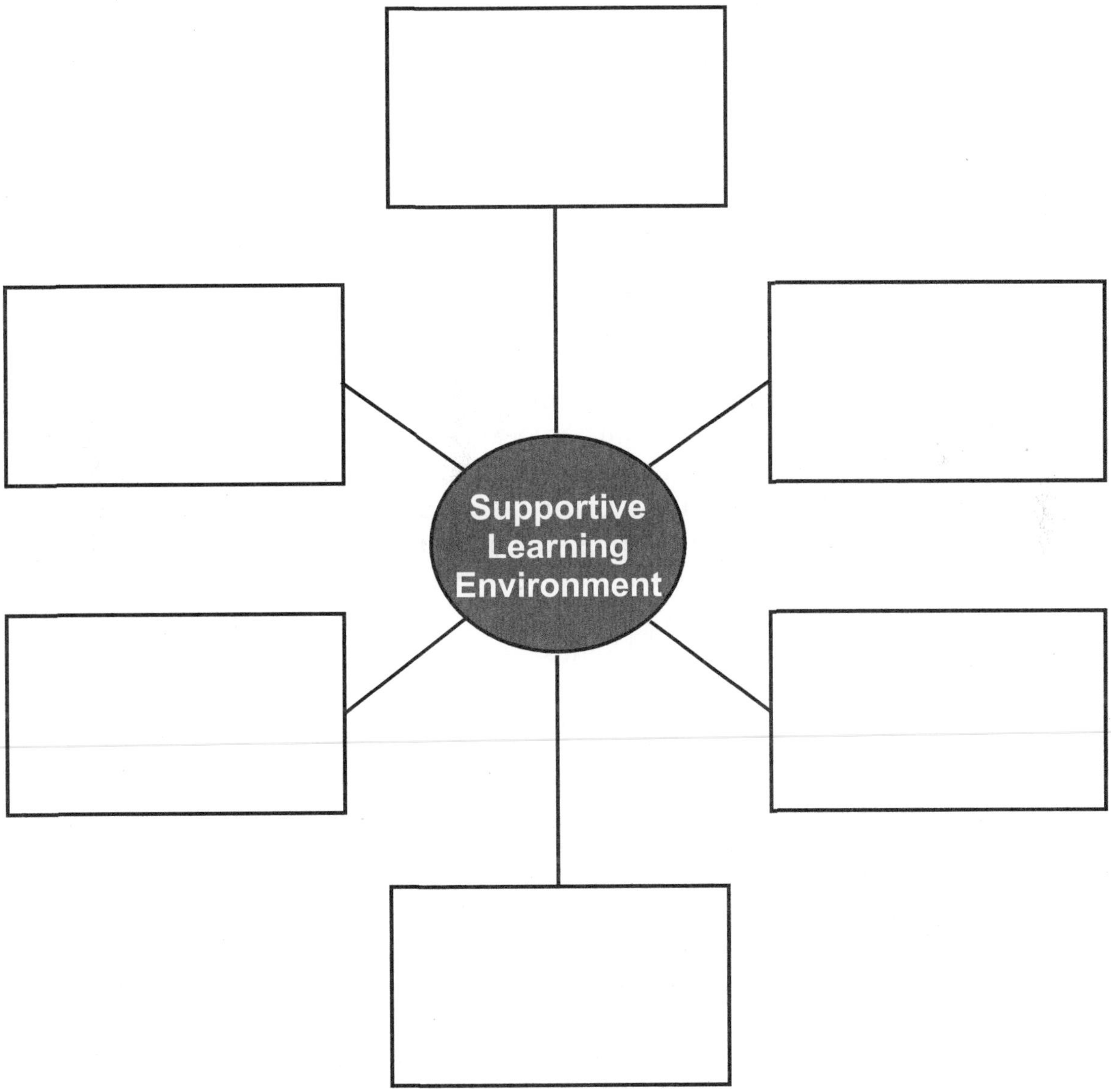

The Language of Results-Based Planning

At this point in the action planning process, many of the best endeavors stall out and come to a grinding halt. Writing a plan using the language of goals, objectives, and performance indicators can begin to decompose into a tortured web of semantics. Language and word choice is far less important than knowing the results you want to accomplish.

The results-based planning model used in this book is a much simpler model. Generically, results-based planning (RBP) is often thought of as planning backward. The process begins with the vision, sometimes referred to as the impact, which envisions a major effect on a maximum number of people throughout the system. Planning is then broken out into smaller increments that measure outcomes and outputs. It delineates strategy or activity selection and then moves to implementation or action steps. Inputs record the human, fiscal, and other resources that will be used to achieve results.

Common Definitions Used in Results-Based Planning

Outcomes refer to the desired long-term results of the project, usually within a two-to-three year time frame. Outcomes are statements that specify what needs to occur to realize the vision or longer-term needs, alleviate deeper problems, or create more lasting systemic changes. By writing the outcomes, the team will often find that one strategy that is selected to alleviate an immediate problem can also be used to develop longer-term outcomes.

Shorter-term or immediate results are generally referred to as *outputs*. Like outcomes, outputs specify the results anticipated at the end of the short-term cycle, generally within six months or a year. Outputs, which have shorter durations for implementation, are meant to deal with the immediate and pressing concerns that confront the team. Outputs relate to outcomes because a series of outputs should develop into a larger outcome. The Action Plan Template (discussed in the next section) demonstrates this dynamic process because several outputs may share the same outcome.

Both outcomes and outputs rely on indicators to benchmark the milestones of success. Indicators must also specify the data sources and information that will produce evidence of success. Indicators attached to outcomes look very much like the long-term goals of the three- and five-year strategic plans of organizations. Indicators attached to outputs are obviously more immediate and produce smaller incremental changes toward deeper systemic changes.

In turn, these results define the activities that the project will engage in. Team members, by engaging in a detailed data-based needs assessment, have already prioritized needs and determined which strategies they believe will most successfully address those identified needs. The action plan details the specific actions required to attain the specified outcomes and immediate outputs, as well as the inputs or human and fiscal resources.

Throughout this process, from visioning forward, the team has these intended outcomes in mind and a picture of what that looks like. The key here is to tease that out in plain, active, alive, and easily decipherable language.

Action Plan Template

There are specific steps to follow when writing your plan. Use the Action Plan Template shown in Figure 6.6 (page 181) to capture all the information on a simple form. Review this form to get a visual image of the process described here. This is a dynamic and flexible process. The plan allows for clarity when moving to implementation, but it should not be viewed as an ironclad contract. It is a method for putting all your ducks in a row and is subject to ongoing revision and refinement. (Refer to Chapter 5 to determine areas of need and corresponding research-based strategies.) Then fill in the information on the Action Plan Template.

- **Area of Need:** The needs the team uncovered in the assessment process have already been prioritized into immediate and longer term needs. This is not an exact science. There may be a few immediate or longer-term priorities that coexist. Often, the longer term priorities can be correlated with the outcomes while the immediate priorities are associated with outputs. Again, use these as guiding suggestions, not as ironclad rules.
- **Strategy:** The team has correlated the identified needs with research-based strategies that have sufficient evidence of success to warrant implementing them. This is

not a haphazard process but one that uses the Seven Key Elements of Supportive Learning Environments as a basis for strategy selection (refer to Figure 3.1, page 38). Effective strategies often have both outcomes and outputs associated with them because they address immediate as well as longer-term needs.

- **Outcomes/Long Term Results:** Record the long-term results that the group is hoping to achieve. (Long-term means two to three years out.) Outcomes produce deeper changes, so they require bigger thinking when determining desired results. Remember to keep the results manageable, not at the level of vision or ultimate impact.
- **Indicators of Success:** How will the team know whether they have achieved these outcomes? What would the specific behaviors and conditions look like? These measures can be qualitative or quantitative and measure effort and effect.
- **Evidence:** What sources of data or information will be used to gather evidence of success at achieving the outcomes and over what period of time? Time frames should be specified.
- **Outputs/Immediate Results:** Record the short-term or immediate results the group is hoping to achieve. These results are short-term or immediate, which means within the next six months to a year. The danger in any plan is stopping at the output stage—this is the quick fix that many ill-conceived plans are built on. Outputs are critically important at alleviating current crises, producing short-term results, and building the small successes into the plan. They act as bridges to the longer-term preventative solutions offered by outcome measures.
- **Indicators of Success:** How will the team know whether they have achieved these outputs? What would the specific behaviors and conditions look like? Again, these measures can be qualitative or quantitative and should measure the quantity and quality of effort and effect.
- **Evidence:** What sources of data or information will be used to gather evidence of success at achieving the outputs and over what period of time? Time frames should be specified.

- **Action Steps:** Break out the implementation into the specific action steps that will be required. These steps outline the actions and inputs that will be necessary to implement the strategy in the short term. Longer-term implementation can be written in as the plan is reviewed and refined. These action steps are not meant to act like an encyclopedia of interventions but as quick, decisive steps in the process of implementation. They should directly relate to the outputs, or short-term goals, rather than the outcomes.
- **Person Responsible:** For each step, specify the person or people who will be responsible for implementing this step. If it is the entire team, hold one person accountable for reporting back and ensuring that the step is completed in a timely manner. This system of accountability embeds the plan within everyone's sphere of influence and is on everyone's radar screen. The plan exists not externally but integrally connected to each person's daily responsibilities. Each person in essence owns the plan.
- **Time Frames:** For each step, specify the time frames for implementing this step. This delineation clarifies the order of interventions and can often determine if something is out of sequence. Keep the timing realistic and adjust it as necessary.

Write a Plan with MERIT

Writing in the language of RBP should be a simple and fast process that avoids the pitfalls of searching vocabulary lists for the proper verbs to use when describing a goal versus an objective. The criteria used in developing goal statements have been much discussed. (A common acronym used in this process is SMART, which stands for Specific, Measurable, Attainable, Realistic, and Time Bound.)

I offer the acronym MERIT, which refers to the criteria used when constructing the language of RBP. The language should be active, purposeful, and alive. It should vividly paint the picture of results. Keep the larger picture in mind while being clear about the specific elements of the intended outcomes, outputs, and coexisting indicators.

MERIT

M = Manageable

Make the strategies, outcomes, and outputs manageable; scale it down to size according to whether it relates to an immediate, a short-term, or a longer-term result. The process is termed *planning backward* because outputs generally come before outcomes. Remind the team that they are building on small successes by keeping the outcomes achievable within two or three years and outputs within six months to a year.

The plan is built by scaffolding the interventions, one upon the other—starting with the most manageable and then moving on in complexity from there. Having a few initial successes will inspire the team with greater confidence to continue innovating, refining, and implementing the plan for continuous improvement rather than trying to accomplish too much with too little and burning out in the process.

One of the key factors in successful change management is applying knowledge of how to sequence interventions or understand the order of change. Sometimes, the most subtle shift can create the very environment that allows innovations to occur. For example, painting over graffiti or brightening a hallway with colorful paint can seem like an insignificant intervention, but the message of pride and respect that it conveys to students, staff, and visitors can begin a sea change in the way people treat each other. Along with a sustained series of interventions, this can pave the way for major changes, built on the small incremental interventions along the way.

E = Effective

The strategies need to be effective at addressing the original issue or problem and satisfactorily resolving it. The team must be clear on the purpose of the selected strategy. It is also important to have evidence of the potential effectiveness of the selected strategies. Research-based practices and other promising practices should form the basis for the strategy selection.

Too often, people implement a program—such as conflict resolution or character education—because they have some vague notion that it will help kids. Even if the program is tested and validated, it is not necessarily the right match for the types of issues of the team. This problem was addressed in the needs-assessment process, with strategies carefully selected from evidence-based practices. In addition, the strategies were correlated with the specific needs and areas for improvement that the team prioritized to ensure effective outcomes.

Continue using the criteria of effectiveness in developing outputs and outcomes. Are these criteria effective at painting the picture and communicating the desired results stemming from the strategy? Are they related to the strategy or do they describe the results of another intervention entirely?

R= Results-Oriented

The plan must provide specific descriptions of the distinct behaviors or conditions that reveal when the desired results are achieved. They should be able to state what the team is trying to achieve. What constitutes good behavior or increased academic achievement? In the words of the song made famous by Roberta Flack; "Trying to keep it real, as compared to what?" How will you know whether it is accomplished?

Avoid fuzzy language and vague or abstract descriptions. Value judgments and vague descriptions such as "good behavior," "effective teaching practices," or "appropriate interventions" have no place in results-oriented language. People say, "I can't explain it, but I'll know it when I see it." That is fine if you're looking for intuitive observations, but it is not appropriate for writing the action plan. The team needs to define the qualities and states that represent successful outcomes, outputs, and indicators. What will convince them that the goal or outcome is attained? What would they like to see more of (or less of)? How can everyone recognize the result? (Mager, 1984b).

Clearly specify the intended outcome, not the process by which the outcome will be achieved. "We will provide every student with an assignment book and personal calendar" describes a process, not a result. The result might sound more like this: "Students will complete homework assignments on time." Depending on the scope of the plan and the underlying need being addressed, providing each student with an assignment book and personal calendar might be found in the action steps or as a single strategy.

I = Integrated

Strategies, outcomes, and outputs should be part of an integrated plan, not stand-alone interventions. The results must be looked at as a whole, as a tapestry woven from multiple strands. The plan itself should be integrated into the overall school improvement plan, not as a separate plan. It should form a cohesive and coherent picture of school improvement in teaching and learning, and it should actively enhance the learning environment.

Single strategies can address multiple needs, multiple outcomes, and multiple outputs. Elements of the plan support and refer to one another. Short-term results build longer-term improvements and systemic changes. The plan should be integrated into the ultimate vision, not exist as a series of isolated strategies addressing disconnected problems.

The idea of sequencing and scaffolding interventions suggests that outcomes and outputs are interrelated and build upon one another. Long- and short-term results can be measured through the achievement of indicators that serve as milestones or benchmarks. Integrate these milestones into the plan in a logical sequence. Charting these developmental markers or benchmarks into the plan and including the corresponding time frames for completion will naturally integrate the separate components and sequence the proper order of change.

T = Targeted

The plan must target a particular population and/or a specific area of need. Being specific about the target of the intervention creates a laser-like focus. How does the team know that it has hit the bull's-eye unless there is a target to aim for? A solid plan is based on a solid needs assessment process, as demonstrated throughout the earlier phases of the planning process.

Targets also refer to the function of measuring outcomes and outputs, so there will be targeted output measures associated with a six-month result and a one-year result, and targeted outcome measures associated with a two-year result and a three-year result. Indicators are used as measures to provide a set of target behaviors, target results, and target dates. Hitting these targets can create the sense of a continued series of small successes. This builds the confidence and trust in the team and in the process; which are so vital for maintaining critical momentum during implementation phases.

Figure 6.6. Action Plan Template

<table>
<tr><td colspan="2">What have we determined are our needs in order of priority?</td><td colspan="2">Organization:</td></tr>
<tr><td colspan="4">Area of Need #</td></tr>
<tr><td colspan="2">How will we address this?</td><td colspan="2">Project Time Frame:</td></tr>
<tr><td colspan="4">Strategy</td></tr>
<tr><td>What long-term results do we hope to achieve?</td><td>How will we know we've been successful?</td><td colspan="2">What sources of data/ information will we gather to show evidence of success?</td></tr>
<tr><td>Outcomes/Long-Term Results</td><td>Indicators of Success</td><td colspan="2">Evidence</td></tr>
<tr><td></td><td></td><td colspan="2"></td></tr>
<tr><td>What immediate results do we hope to achieve?</td><td>How will we know we've been successful?</td><td colspan="2">What sources of data/ information will we gather to show evidence of success?</td></tr>
<tr><td>Outputs/Results</td><td>Indicators of Success</td><td colspan="2">Evidence</td></tr>
<tr><td></td><td></td><td colspan="2"></td></tr>
<tr><td colspan="2">Action Steps: Implementing the Strategy</td><td>Person Responsible</td><td>Time Frames</td></tr>
<tr><td></td><td></td><td></td><td></td></tr>
<tr><td></td><td></td><td></td><td></td></tr>
<tr><td></td><td></td><td></td><td></td></tr>
<tr><td></td><td></td><td></td><td></td></tr>
<tr><td></td><td></td><td></td><td></td></tr>
<tr><td></td><td></td><td></td><td></td></tr>
<tr><td></td><td></td><td></td><td></td></tr>
</table>

Figure 6.6. Action Plan Template (continues)

<table>
<tr><th colspan="3">Exercise: Case Scenario: Sample Action Plan for Hillside High School</th></tr>
<tr><td colspan="3">Remember the Hillside High School team from Chapter 5?
Compare your Action Plan Template to the one below.</td></tr>
<tr><td colspan="2">What have we determined are our needs in order of priority?</td><td>Organization:
Hillside High School</td></tr>
<tr><td colspan="3">Area of Need # 1: 9th graders perceive a lack of caring relationships, sense of community bonding, and school connectedness.</td></tr>
<tr><td colspan="2">How will we address this?</td><td>Project Time Frame:
6/04–6/07</td></tr>
<tr><td colspan="3">Strategy: Establish an advisory program for the 9th grade.</td></tr>
<tr><td>What long-term results do we hope to achieve?</td><td>How will we know we've been successful?</td><td>What sources of data/ information will we gather to show evidence of success?</td></tr>
<tr><td>Outcomes/Long-Term Results</td><td>Indicators of Success</td><td>Evidence</td></tr>
<tr><td>Decrease in disproportionate numbers of students of color, poor, special ed., and/or limited English proficient students in issues of truancy, dropping out, discipline referrals, and low academic achievement</td><td>Higher rates of attendance over next three yearsHigher academic achievement increase in numbers of students in levels 3 and 4Increased school completion ratesDecreased number of referrals from students</td><td>Attendance records:
04–05, 05–06, 06–07
State assessment scores:
04–05, 05–06, 06–07
School dropout rates:
04–05, 05–06, 06–07
Referrals:
04–05, 05–06, 06–07</td></tr>
<tr><td>What immediate results do we hope to achieve?</td><td>How will we know we've been successful?</td><td>What sources of data/ information will we gather to show evidence of success?</td></tr>
<tr><td>Outputs/Results</td><td>Indicators of Success</td><td>Evidence</td></tr>
<tr><td>Incoming 9th graders report high levels of school connection over next year</td><td>Annual increase of 25% of students who report greater sense of school connection</td><td>Student surveys: administered 2x per year over next year</td></tr>
</table>

Action Steps: Implementing the Strategy	Person Responsible	Time Frames
1. Structure 9th graders into daily homeroom advisory groups by using class lists.	Liz and A. Principal	By 7/04
2. Locate a trainer to train teachers to act as advisors.	Bill W.	By 8/04
3. Schedule training and orientation sessions for teachers.	Janeh	By 9/04
4. Conduct orientation session for teachers.	Liz, Bill, A.P., and Janeh	By 9/04
5. Conduct training of teachers.	Trainer + Team	9/04–10/04
6. Begin advisory program for 9th graders during daily homeroom class.	All 9th grade teachers	11/04

7

Continuous Assessment and Improvement: Are We There Yet?

We must not cease from our exploration and the end of all our exploring will be when we arrive where we began and to know the place for the first time.

TS Eliot

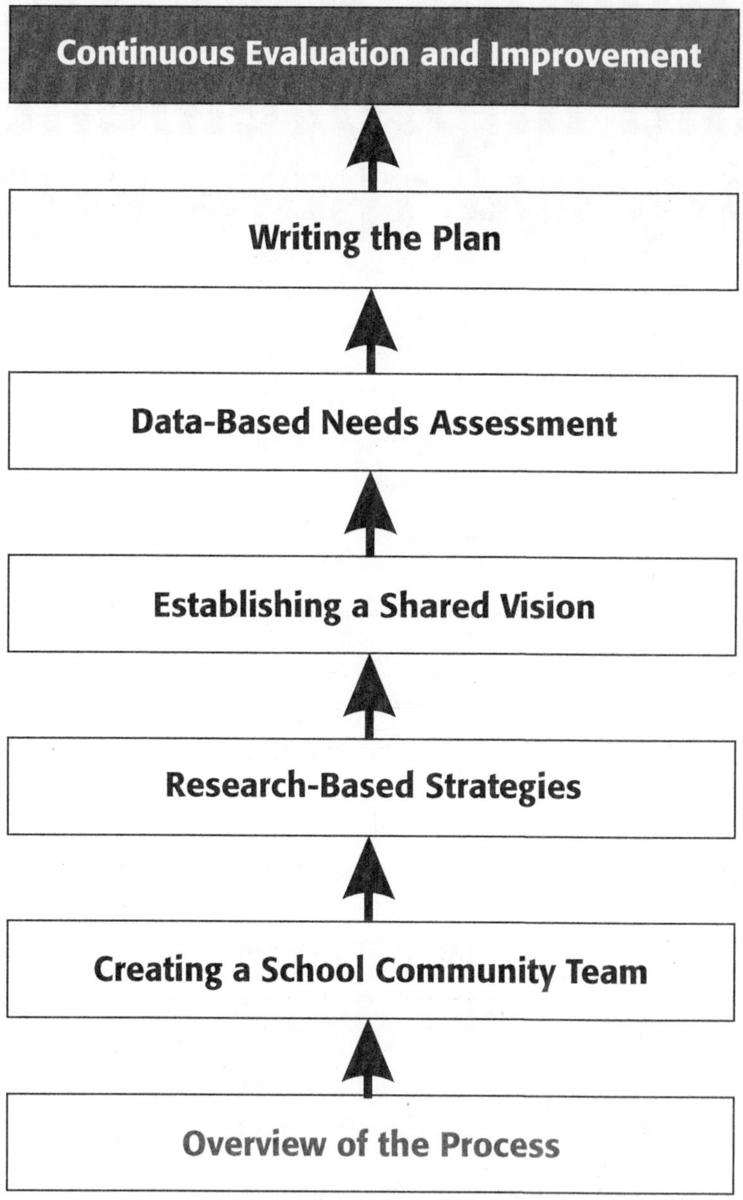
Continuous Evaluation and Improvement
Writing the Plan
Data-Based Needs Assessment
Establishing a Shared Vision
Research-Based Strategies
Creating a School Community Team
Overview of the Process

Are We There Yet?

Those of us who have traveled on long road trips as children or traveled with our own children or grandchildren remember this refrain: Are We There Yet? Usually this question is uttered within the first hour or two after embarking on a three-day trip. For my family growing up in New York, one of us was sure to say it right after crossing the George Washington Bridge into New Jersey on our way to visit my grandmother in Florida. The response was always the same: Not Quite There Yet.

The idea of action planning bears a striking similarity to the Not Quite There Yet response. In fact, if done well, the team soon realizes that there is no *there*—only movement toward the ultimate vision and continuous improvement all along the way. As the team develops expertise in implementing, evaluating, and refining the plan, it becomes efficient at sustaining successful interventions and improving on existing or faulty processes or practices.

Cyclical Nature of Change

The continuous improvement process allows us to view the plan as a living document, not as a static, fixed entity. The team will continue to tweak and adjust the plan through continuous refinements and revisions based on frequent data-driven assessments of what's working and what's not. This ongoing refinement process is a spiraling cycle, attesting to the cyclical nature of change. The team moves in and out of earlier phases of data-driven inquiry and needs assessment at higher and higher levels of inquiry and involvement. Throughout the evaluation and monitoring process, the team continues to collect quantitative and qualitative data to inform process and outcome evaluation, and reuses familiar tools for new and evolving assessment purposes.

Ongoing communication and dialogue are central in the continuous refinement of the plan. Questions breed answers and solutions that in turn raise more questions. This discovery process creates energy and excitement, stimulates discussion and exploration, engages intellectual curiosity, and becomes integral to the ongoing process of planning and implementation. Communication with stakeholders is a critical component of this spiraling feedback and discovery process.

Unlike the game of Monopoly, in which players are sometimes instructed to "Go straight to jail, do not pass Go, do not collect $200," the team circles the board and revisits questions, tools, and processes in a spiraling and evolving process of creating depth and breadth to the interventions. Although minor setbacks are likely to occur, the change process does not go around in circles; it loops in increasingly complex orbits, allowing higher and higher levels of innovation and improvement to occur.

Ongoing Evaluation Mechanisms Used in the Planning Process

Many people associate evaluation with the end of a process, a way to prove it is working. Evaluation is actually part of the ongoing process. The team has engaged in various forms of evaluation and assessment throughout the entire action planning process. When developing a school community team, members were asked to critically examine and evaluate the existing alliances and connections and develop strategies for extending the network into the community. This is a form of quality improvement using tools of evaluation. Developing the vision asked team members to evaluate contrasting versions of the future to select and agree on one that would guide the team, another form of quality improvement

Becoming familiar with the research-based elements of supportive learning environments ensured that team members used rigorous criteria in seeking quality solutions to address their needs. This process required critical evaluation, assessment, and understanding of the methods and strategies used in developing learning communities.

The needs assessment process is probably the most obvious use of data to evaluate and inform decisions. The team used many mechanisms to evaluate personal observations and to determine and extend hunches, hypotheses, and guesses about problem causation. Data sources were used as evidence of these hypotheses. These same tools and data sources can be used in multiple ways to inform an ongoing evaluation of the project throughout the many phases of implementation.

The writing of the plan called for delineating success by developing milestones, indicators, and measures of results. The team had to cite data sources that could be gathered to provide evidence of successful implementation. Many of the same tools were used in the needs assessment process. These are examples of using a broad variety of evaluation mechanisms on an ongoing basis.

Quantitative and Qualitative Measures

The team has been using and will continue to use a variety of quantitative and qualitative assessment tools throughout the process (refer to Chapter 5). Examples of the quantitative measures include attendance records, discipline referrals, school completion rates, free and reduced lunch rates, census data, parent contacts with the school, number of extracurricular activities student are involved in, and afterschool and community resources available to students. Also included, of course, is a wide variety of tools that capture academic achievement: state assessments, regents, report cards, homework assignments, and so on.

This team will continue to examine or mine the data in a variety of ways to tell different and deeper stories. Disaggregated data showing subgroup populations according to race, ethnicity, gender, socioeconomic status, and level of English proficiency will continue to be tracked for changes in student achievement and behavioral performance. This tracking yields valuable information over time about trends and underlying patterns that need examining.

Qualitative measures will continue to be gathered by the team in the forms of student, parent, and staff surveys; forums; focus groups; individual or online interviews; teacher observations of student behaviors; entrance and exit interviews; and additional methods the team may devise for gathering important information. These tools capture the personal observations, attitudes, beliefs, and feelings of participants in ways that qualitative measures cannot do.

All these tools have been part of ongoing assessments throughout the process. The team will use these same tools as they begin to chart the progress of the interventions in delivering the desired results. These tools, both quantitative and qualitative, were cited in the evidence section for indicators of progress in achieving the desired results.

Assessing Progress: Process Evaluation

Moving into the implementation phases of the project, the team needs to be vigilant about meeting on a monthly or biweekly basis. It is important to continuously assess the progress toward implementing the plan and ensuring that the progress and momentum continues. The Action Plan Template should be used as the primary document or blueprint. This plan or blueprint serves as a neon road marker, delineating the steps and timelines along the way. The group needs to evaluate how well it is meeting the timelines and following the action steps. The action steps and timelines, in turn, need to be checked and adjusted for accuracy. If the project is falling behind by two weeks, the plan should be adjusted accordingly to reflect the change in time frame.

Allow for a margin of error as you continue with the implementation process. If delays are occurring less than 25% of the time, the team should not spend a lot of time exploring the reasons for the delay. Instead, it should proactively work to resolve the issues as quickly as possible. However, if the team is consistently missing its target dates, the group needs to figure out how often this occurs: 30% of the time, 40% of the time? Slow the process down and explore why this is occurring to make the appropriate course corrections.

Process monitoring can be valuable for identifying unanticipated barriers or obstacles in the change effort. These delays should be expected, but cannot always be accurately pinpointed, so careful monitoring of the plan can help highlight these obstacles before they become major stumbling blocks. The team should remain committed and flexible when refining and adjusting the schedule of implementation, but should try not to substantively alter the major components of the plan. To use one of my favorite analogies, the team is still headed for California, but it may have to make a slight detour, get off the highway at a rest stop, and check its maps before resuming the journey.

Monitoring Progress of the Interventions

One of the most difficult tasks of evaluation is monitoring the progress of the interventions in producing the desired results. Ongoing data collection and evaluation, as written into the Action Plan Template and specified in the indicators and evidence, are the primary tools to assist in this process. The team needs to look critically at what is working well and what is not working as successfully. Be careful not to form premature judgments and conclusions about the nature of the success, or lack thereof, of the interventions.

As the team meets on a regular basis, assign data collection to one or two members of the team. The team needs to gather evidence on a continuing basis and plan intentional evaluation sessions to explore the data and determine progress toward success. These sessions should be incorporated into the monthly meetings throughout the project. Short-term output indicators are usually measured monthly. Longer-term outcome indicators are generally measured no sooner than six months from the start of implementation and then every six months to one year afterward.

The team critically evaluates and monitors the indicators and evidence connected to the outcomes and outputs. In the process, the team asks itself a host of questions, stemming from and directly related to the intended results recorded in the plan. Has student achievement increased? Has attendance increased? Have discipline referrals decreased? Is the advisory program really affecting and creating favorable student attitudes toward the school? These are not new questions. They are the very questions embedded in the plan in the form of indicators. Examine the evidence to ascertain the success in reaching these indicators.

It is generally difficult to chart immediate changes in behavior. Sometimes, an examination of the data may not always present a clear picture. For example, there is an old adage in healing that says when you recover from an illness you tend to feel your worst—just as you are on the verge of getting better. Put another way, things usually get worse before they get better.

The same is true for systemic change. Whenever an innovation is introduced, there is often a lag time before it catches on, before people gain familiarity or become comfortable with the change. In the interim, there may often be a slight increase in the old and undesirable behaviors before the trend shifts toward the more favorable, healthier results.

For example, discipline referrals often increase when the system goes through a deliberate change in response. People notice behaviors and pay more attention rather than ignore them. As people learn more positive methods of interaction, the discipline referrals eventually decrease, signaling the shift and adoption of new behaviors.

Be patient with change, especially change in behavior. Results do not always show up right away, which is why multiple assessment measures are most effective at tracking changes. Using quantitative measures derived from surveys, forums, and focus groups can yield rich and immediate sources of information, long before the changes may show up qualitatively as behavioral shifts.

In the best of all possible worlds, explore options of using an outside evaluator in this process. This is not to suggest that the team cannot conduct evaluations of the project on its own, using the plan itself as a guide. The process is relatively straightforward and simple, and the team should have no problem becoming adept at self-monitoring and evaluation. However, by now the team has no doubt also become quite good at leveraging expertise from a variety of sources. It might be helpful to find and use the expertise of an outside evaluator to conduct or advise the team, particularly early on in the evaluation process. Area colleges and universities can be helpful in supplying a graduate student or another form of student intern who can assist with conducting formal evaluations. Use higher education partnerships and incorporate the plan into existing evaluation efforts that might be occurring with these partnerships.

Self Assessment and Reflection

The team may want to provide opportunities to engage in self-assessment; using a beginning assessment once the plan is developed and following up with a mid-year and an end of the year assessment (see Figure 7.1, page 194). It is a good opportunity to poll team members about how well they think the plan is addressing the core needs related to teaching and learning. It allows for some honest discussion and reflection about the process itself. During the self-assessment, members can give opinions about what they feel is going well and what is not going as well in terms of the development of the plan.

Figure 7.1. Self-Assessments

1 = Not evident in my school 2 = Somewhat or occasionally evident in my school 3 = Consistently evident in my school 4 = Consistently evident and provides an excellent exemplar				
Self-Assessment: Beginning of the Year	**1**	**2**	**3**	**4**
Plan is integrated with existing (school improvements and/or strategic) plan. Plan is based on a data inquiry process that includes input from multiple constituents and data sources. Plan builds on existing strengths within the school. Plan addresses needs that interfere with learning. Plan correlates needs to research based strategies and/or promising practices to improve fundamental barriers to learning. Plan sequences the implementation of strategies for maximum effectiveness. Plan assesses the outcomes using supportive evidence. Plan shows measurable success in achieving outcomes.				
Self-Assessment: Mid-Year	**1**	**2**	**3**	**4**
Plan is integrated with existing (school improvements and/or strategic) plan. Plan is based on a data inquiry process that includes input from multiple constituents and data sources. Plan builds on existing strengths within the school. Plan addresses needs that interfere with learning. Plan correlates needs to research-based strategies and/or promising practices to improve fundamental barriers to learning. Plan sequences the implementation of strategies for maximum effectiveness. Plan assesses the outcomes using supportive evidence. Plan shows measurable success in achieving outcomes.				
Self-Assessment: End of the Year	**1**	**2**	**3**	**4**
Plan is integrated with existing (school improvements and/or strategic) plan. Plan is based on a data inquiry process that includes input from multiple constituents and data sources. Plan builds on existing strengths within the school. Plan addresses needs that interfere with learning. Plan correlates needs to research-based strategies and/or promising practices to improve fundamental barriers to learning. Plan sequences the implementation of strategies for maximum effectiveness. Plan assesses the outcomes using supportive evidence. Plan shows measurable success in achieving outcomes.				

This process differs from the actual evaluation of the Action Plan in that it allows for honest critique of the plan as a whole, not simply the implementation process. It can be helpful to ensure that the plan stays connected to the core goals of teaching and learning within the school. Perhaps most importantly, it allows the team to take a step back from the hard work of implementation and reflect on the plan itself as a living document. It allows for personal reflection and the continued building of trust and a sense of collective purpose that binds the group together.

The team may choose to develop its own self-assessment tool and create a rubric that allows members to envision what the particular strategies look like at level 4: the exemplar of excellence. This can refresh the group's vision and motivate the group to strive toward its goals.

The most important consideration throughout the process is to keep the focus on improving the learning environment in tangible ways and providing measurable outcomes of that progress. All efforts to create a self-assessment tool and reflection time are helpful to keep the team on track and in alignment with its core goals and mission.

Creating a Positive Feedback Loop

In any change process, you must always anticipate some resistance. The law of entropy says that things will deteriorate if left to their natural state. Overcoming inertia, let alone the entropic process of deterioration, takes enormous resolve and continued momentum. Expect delays. Expect setbacks. Expect resistance. Use these things as positive indicators that change is being enacted.

Ongoing communication is critical for ensuring success throughout the project. It is particularly important during the early phases of recruitment and team formation, and later on in the implementation and evaluation phase. Informing constituents about the ongoing nature of the project can be accomplished through a concerted public relations campaign. This should not be a complicated new endeavor, but should build on existing channels of communication. Assign a member of the team to serve as communications liaison from the project team to the larger school community. There are a host of existing mechanisms that can and should be used in the process (see Figure 7.2. page 196).

Figure 7.2. Communication and Feedback Loops

Use existing mechanisms to create an ongoing flow of communication and feedback loops between the project team and the larger school community. The following are suggestions for existing channels of communication.

- Incorporate a positive public relations blurb about the project into:
    - School newsletters
    - PTA newsletters
    - Newsletters of community partners such as community-based organizations
    - Newsletters of faith-based organizations
    - Local radio spots reserved for free public service announcements
    - Local newspapers
    - School web site
- Publicly display your meeting schedule in:
    - Newsletters (see first section)
    - Local radio announcements
    - Local newspaper calendars of events
    - Local cable TV calendars of events
    - School web site
- Make a brief presentation about the project at:
    - Every faculty meeting
    - Every school improvement meeting
    - Monthly school board meeting
- Use local media outlets to conduct interviews with stakeholders about the project
- Publish positive stories from parents and students about the project
- Create a Success Story of the Week on the school web site or electronic bulletin board
- Use local media outlets to conduct a "How are We Doing?" write-in campaign

The team might want to devise a few simple tools to measure the progress of implementation and assess the level of acceptance or resistance to change. For example, asking student, parents and community members to rate the school by having a "How are We Doing?" write-in campaign can serve many purposes. It creates an immediate feedback loop and allows the team to get a flavor for how the intervention and project are being viewed. This information can in turn inform the team's efforts, explain possible delays, and help the team become more proactive in overcoming possible resistances.

Important public relations functions can be served by employing a strategy like a "How are We Doing?" write-in campaign. Using local media channels such as the local newspaper or radio, in addition to the more traditional school venues, can be effective at communicating that the school is serious about inviting input. It enables constituents to participate actively in the process and can minimize resistance to change efforts. It also elicits valuable information for guiding ongoing assessments and interventions.

Inviting students, parents, and others to share positive stories and experiences about the project can be instrumental toward building solid community support for ongoing implementation. This is an intentional process and is substantially different from conducting random interviews for assessment purposes. There is nothing wrong with seeding positive descriptions of the project all around town. View it as an intentional opportunity to capitalize on success!

Additional References

Element 1: Safety of the Physical Plant

Trump, K. S. (1998, June–July). Crisis in the classroom: Can your schools' security pass the exam? *Updating School Board Policies, 29*(3), 1–4.

U. S. Department of Education. (2000). *Safeguarding our children: An action guide.* Washington DC: Author.

Element 2: Shared Leadership Practices

Martel, L. D. (1993). Building a learning community: School leaders and their organizations need to share a vision to challenge all young minds. *School Administrator, 50*(6), 22–27.

Wald, P. J., & Castleberry, M. S. (2000). *Educators as learners: Creating a professional learning community in your school.* Alexandria, VA: Association for Supervision and Curriculum Development.

Element 3: Structured Personalized Learning Environments

Small Schools

Newmann, F. M., & Wehlage, G. G. (1995). *Successful school restructuring.* Madison: Center on Organization and Restructuring of Schools, School of Education, University of Wisconsin–Madison.

Seidman, E., Allen, L., Aber, J. L., Mitchell, C., & Feinman, J. (1994). The impact of school transitions in early adolescence on the self-system and perceived social context of poor urban youth. *Child Development, 65,* 507–522.

Schools Within Schools

Alspaugh, J. W., & Harting, R. D. (1997). Effects of team teaching on the transition to middle school. *ERS Spectrum, 15*(1), (pp. 9–14).

Advisory Programs

Black, S. (2002, October). Getting advisories right. *American School Board Journal, 189*(10), (pp. 48–49).

Goldberg, M. F. (2001). *How to design an advisory system for a secondary school.* Alexandria, VA.: Association for Supervision and Curriculum Development.

Transition Programs

Hertzog, C. J., Morgan, P. L., Diamond, P. A., & Walker, M. J. (1996). Transition to high school: A look at student perceptions. *Becoming, 7*(2), 6–8.

Mac Iver, D. J., & Epstein, J. L. (1991). Responsive practices in the middle grades: Teacher teams, advisory groups, remedial instruction, and school transition programs. *American Journal of Education, 99*(4), 587–622.

Afterschool and Extended Day Programs

Hamilton, L. S., & Klein, S. P. (1998). *Achievement test score gains among participants in the foundations school-age enrichment program.* Santa Monica, CA: RAND Corporation.

Huang, D., Gribbons, B., Kim, K. S., & Lee, C. (May 2000). *The impact of the LA's BEST after school program on subsequent student achievement and performance.* Los Angeles: University of California, Los Angeles.

Tierney, J. (2000). *Making a Difference: An Impact Study of Big Brothers/Big Sisters.* Philadelphia: Public/Private Ventures.

Continuum of Supports

Adelman, H. S., & Taylor, L. (1997). Addressing barriers to learning: Beyond school-linked services and full service schools. *American Journal of Orthopsychiatry, 67*, 408–421.

Adelman, H. S., & Taylor, L. (2000). Looking at school health and school reform policy through the lens of addressing barriers to learning. *Children's Services: Social Policy, Research, and Practice, 3*, 117–132.

Duke, D. L. (1990). School organization, leadership, and student behavior. In O. C. Moles (Ed.), *Student discipline strategies: Research and practice* (pp. 31-62). Albany, NY: State University of New York Press.

Felner, R. D., Brand, S., Adan, A. M., & Mulhall, P. F. (1993). Restructuring the ecology of the school as an approach to prevention during school transitions: Longitudinal follow-ups and extensions of the School Transitional Environment Project (STEP). *Prevention in Human Services, 10*(2), 103–136.

Element 4: Student-Centered Learning Environments

Student-Centered Instruction and Assessment Practices

Bandura, A., & Schunk, D. H. (1981). Cultivating competence, self-efficacy, and intrinsic interest through proximal self-motivation. *Journal of Personality and Social Psychology, 41*, 569–578.

Miller, D., & Kelley, M. L. (1994). The use of goal setting and contingency contracting for improving children's homework performance. *Journal of Applied Behavioral Analysis, 27*(1), 73–84.

Morgan, M. (1985). Self-monitoring of attained subgoals in private study. *Journal of Educational Psychology, 77*(6), 623–630.

Trammel, D. L., Schloss, P. J., & Alper, S. (1994). Using self-recording and graphing to increase completion of homework assignments. *Journal of Learning Disabilities, 27*(2), 75–81.

Wiggins, G. (1993). *Assessing student performance: Exploring the purpose and limits of testing*. San Francisco: Jossey-Bass.

Cooperative Learning

Lou, Y., Abrami, P. C., Spence, J. C., Paulsen, C., Chambers, B., & d'Appolonio, S. (1996). Within-class grouping: A meta-analysis. *Review of Educational Research, 66*(4), 423–458.

Community Service and Service Learning

Bricker, D. C. (1989). *Classroom life as civic education: Individual achievement and student cooperation in schools*. New York: Teachers College Press.

Moore, C. W., & Allen, J. P. (1996). The effects of volunteering on the young volunteer. *Journal of Primary Prevention, 17*(2), 231–258.

Staub, E. (1981). Promoting positive behavior in schools, in other educational settings, and in the home, In Rushton, J. & Sorrentino, R. (Eds.), *Altruism and behavior: Social, personality, and developmental perspectives*(109–133). Hillsdale, NJ: Lawrence Erlbaum.

Individualized Performance Feedback

Urdan, T., Midgley, C., & Anderman, E. M. (1998). The role of classroom goal structure in students' use of self-handicapping strategies. *American Educational Research Journal, 35*(1), 101–122.

Multicultural Competence

Gilligan, C. (1982). *In a different voice*. Cambridge MA: Harvard University Press.

Kozol, J. (1989). *Rachel and her children: Homeless families in America*. New York: Fawcett Columbine.

Kozol, J. (1995). *Amazing grace: The lives of children and the conscience of a nation*. New York: Crown Publishers.

Phinney, J. S. (1990). Ethnic identity in adolescents and adults: Review of research. *Psychological Bulletin, 108*, 499–514.

Phinney, J. S. (1991). Ethnic identity and self-esteem: A review and integration. *Hispanic Journal of Behavioral Sciences, 13*, 193–206.

Phinney, J. S. (1992). The multigroup ethnic identity measure: A new scale for use with diverse groups. *Journal of Adolescent Research, 7*, 156–176.

Phinney, J. S., & Devich-Navarro, M. (1997). Variations of bicultural identification among African-American and Mexican-American adolescents. *Journal of Research on Adolescence, 7*(1), 3–32.

West, Cornel. (1993). *Race matters* . Boston: Beacon Press.

Element 5: Caring Relationships and Sense of Community

High Expectations

Bamburg, J. (1994). *Raising expectations to improve student learning*. Oak Brook, IL: North Central Regional Educational Laboratory.

Brophy, J. (1986). *On motivating students*. East Lansing: Institute for Research on Teaching, Michigan State University.

Eccles, J. S., Early, D., Fraser, K., Belansky, E., & McCarthy, K. (1997). The relation of connection, regulation, and support for autonomy to adolescents' functioning. *Journal of Adolescent Research, 12*, 263–286.

Shouse, R. C. (1996). Academic press and sense of community: conflict, congruence, and implications for student achievement. *Social Psychology of Education, 1*(1): 47–68.

Support from Adults

Anderson, J. F., & Anderson, P. A. (1987). Never smile until Christmas? Casting doubt on an old myth. *Journal of Thought; 22*, 57–61.

Felner, R. D., Jackson, A. W., Kasak, D., Mulhall, P. F., Brand, S., & Flowers, N. (1997). The impact of school reform for the middle years: Longitudinal study of a network engaged in Turning Points-based comprehensive school transformation. *Phi Delta Kappan, 78*, 528–532, 541–550.

Ginott, H. G. (1972). *Teacher and child*. New York: Macmillan.

Rosenfeld, L. B., Richman, J. M., Bowen, G. L. (2000). Social support networks and school outcomes: the centrality of the teacher. *Child and Adolescent Social Work Journal, 17*(3): 205–226.

Teachers' Sense of Community

Lee, V. E., Bryk, A. S., Smith, J. B. (1993). The organization of effective secondary schools. In L. Darling-Hammond (Ed.), *Review of research in education, Vol. 19* (pp. 171–267). Washington, DC: American Educational Research Association.

School Community and Positive School Climate

Coker, J. K., & Borders, L. D. (2001). An analysis of environmental and social factors affecting adolescent problem drinking. *Journal of Counseling and Development, 79,* 200–208.

Learning First Alliance. (2001). *Every child learning: Safe and supportive schools.* Alexandria, VA: Association for Supervision and Curriculum Development.

Solomon, D., Battistich, V., Watson, M., Schaps, E., & Lewis, C. (2000). A six-district study of educational change: Direct and mediated effects of the Child Development Project. *Social Psychology of Education, 4,* 3–51.

Students Feel a Sense of Bonding and Belonging

Marks, H.M. (2000). Student engagement in instructional activity: patterns in the elementary, middle and high school years. *American Educational Research Journal, 37*(1); 153–184.

Skinner, E. A. (1995). *Perceived control, motivation and coping.* Thousand Oaks, CA: Sage.

Academically Engaged

Finn, J. D. (1989). Withdrawing from school. *Review of Educational Research, 59,* 117–142.

Jenkins, J. E. (1996). The influence of peer affiliation and student activities on adolescent drug involvement. *Adolescence, 31,* 297–306.

Jessor, R., Van Den Bos, J., Vanderryn, J., Costa, F. M., & Turbin, M. S. (1995). Protective factors in adolescent problem behavior: moderator effects and development change. *Developmental Psychology, 31,* 923–933.

Optimistic Attitude Toward School

Stevenson, H., & Stigler, J. (1992). *The learning gap: Why our schools are failing and what we can learn from Japanese and Chinese education.* New York: Summit Books.

Positive Peer Relations

Mattern, C., & Nakagawa, K. (2003). Segregating students on the margin: Peer relationships in alternative charter high schools. *Current Issues in Education*. 6(16). Available online at: http://cie.ed.asu.edu/volume6/number16/

Bullying and Teasing

Bandura, A. (1973). *Aggression: A social learning analysis.* Englewood Cliffs, NJ: Prentice Hall.

Garbarino, J. (1999). *Lost boys: Why our sons turn violent and how we can save them*. New York: Anchor Books.

Garbarino, J., & Abramowitz, R. (1992). Sociocultural risk and opportunity. In J. Garbarino, (Ed.), *Children and families in the social environment* (2nd ed., pp. 35–70). New York: Aldine De Gruyter.

Pipher, M. (1994). *Reviving Ophelia: Saving the selves of adolescent girls*. New York: Putnam.

Pollack, W. (1998). *Real boys: Rescuing our sons from the myths of boyhood*. New York: Henry Holt.

Pollack, W., & Shuster, T. (2000). *Real boys' voices*. New York: Random House.

Pollack, W., & Cushman, K. (2001). *Real boys workbook*. New York: Villard.

Prothrow-Stith, D. (1991). *Deadly consequences*. New York: HarperCollins.

Prothrow-Stith, D., Spivak, H., & Hausman, A. J. (1987). The violence prevention project: A public health approach. *Science, Technology, and Human Values, 12*, 67–69.

Social and Emotional Needs

Elias, M. J., Gara, M. A., Schuyler, T. F., Branden-Muller, L. R., & Sayette, M. A. (1991). The promotion of social competence: Longitudinal study of a preventive school-based program. *American Journal of Orthopsychiatry, 61*(3), 409–417.

Erikson, E.H. (1968). *Identity: Youth and crisis*. New York: Norton

Kohlberg, L. (1981). *Essays on moral development, Vol. 1.* . New York: Harper& Row.

Piaget, J. (1952). *The origins of intelligence in children*. New York: International Universities Press.

Piaget, J. (1965). *The moral judgment of the child*. New York: Free Press.

Element 6: Schoolwide Positive Discipline and Self-Management Practices

Social Skills

Ellickson, P. L., Bell, R. M. & McGuigan, K. (1993). Preventing adolescent drug use: Long-term results of a junior high program. *American Journal of Public Health, 83*(6), 856–861.

Greenberg, M. T., Kusche, C. A., Cook, E. T., & Quamma, J. P. (1995). Promoting emotional competence in school-aged children: The effects of the PATHS Curriculum. *Development in Psychopathology, 7*, 117–136.

Tolan, P. H., & Guerra, N. G. (1998). *What works in reducing adolescent violence: An empirical review of the field*. Boulder, CO: Center for the Study and Prevention of Violence.

Weissberg, R. P., & Greenberg, M. T. (1997). School and community competence-enhancement and prevention programs. In W. Damon (Series Ed.), I. E. Siegel, and K. A. Renninger (Vol. Eds.), *Handbook of child psychology: Vol 4. Child psychology in practice* (5th ed., pp. 877–954). New York: Wiley.

Positive Classroom Management

Deci, E. L., Spiegel, N. H., Ryan, R. M., Koestner, R., & Kauffman, M. (1982). Effects of performance standards on teaching styles: Behavior of controlling teachers. *Journal of Educational Psychology, 74*, 852–859.

Raffini, J. (1993) *Winners without losers: Structures and strategies for increasing student motivation to learn*. Boston: Allyn & Bacon

Wang, M., Haertel, G., & Walberg, H. (1998). Models of reform: A comparative guide. *Educational Leadership, 55*(7), 66–71.

Equitable Discipline Policy

McCarthy, J. D., & Hoge, D R., (1987). The social construction of school punishment: Racial disadvantage out of universalistic process. *Social Forces, 65*(4), 1101–1120.

Element 7: Active Student, Staff, Family, and Community Involvement

Staff Involvement

Becker, B. J., & Riel, M. M. (1999). *Teacher professionalism, school work culture and the emergence of constructivist-compatible pedagogies.* Presented at annual meeting of American Educational Research Association, Montreal.

Smylie, M. A., & Hart, A. W. (1999). School leadership for teacher learning and change: A human and social capital development perspective. In. J. Murphy & K. S. Louis (Eds.), *Handbook of research on educational administration* (2nd ed., pp. 421–441). San Francisco: Jossey-Bass.

Active Student Involvement

AEC Foundation. (1995, August). *The path of most resistance: Reflections on lessons learned from New Futures.* Baltimore: Author.

Deci, E. L., Vallerand, R. J., Pelletier, L. G., Ryan, R. M. (1991). Motivation and education: The self-determination perspective. *Educational Psychology, 26*(3–4), 325–346.

Roth, J., Brooks-Gunn, J., Galen, B., Murray, L., Silverman, P., Liu, H., Man, D. & Foster, W. (1997). *Promoting healthy adolescence: Youth development frameworks and programs.* New York: Center for Children and Families.

Ryan, A. M., Grolnick, W. (1984). Origins and pawns in the classroom: Self-report and projective assessments of individual differences in children's perceptions. *Journal of Personality and Social Psychology, 50*, 500–558.

Student Participation in Extracurricular Activities

U.S. Department of Education, National Center for Education Statistics. (2001). *Digest of Education Statistics, 2000.* Washington DC: Author.

Support from Family

Baumrind, D. (1971). Current patterns of parental authority. *Developmental Psychology Monographs, 4*, 1–102.

Baumrind, D. (1991). The influence of parenting style on adolescent competence and substance use. *Journal of Early Adolescence, 11*, 56–95.

Brandt, R. (1989). On parents and schools: A conversation with Joyce Epstein. *Educational Leadership, 47*(2): 24–27.

Comer, J. P. (1984). Home-school relationships as they affect the academic success of children. *Education and Urban Society, 71*, 323–337.

Comer, J. P. (1986). Parent participation in the schools. *Phi Delta Kappan, 67*, 442–446.

Comer, J. P. (1988a). Educating poor minority children. *Scientific American, 259*(5), 42–48.

Comer, J. P. (1988b). Is parenting essential to good teaching? *National Education Association Today, 6*(6), 34–40.

Steinberg, L., Darling, N. E., Fletcher, A. C., Brown, B. B., & Dornbusch, S. M. (1995). Authoritative parenting and adolescent adjustment: An ecological journey. In P. Moen, G. H. Elder, Jr., & K. Luscher (Eds.), *Examining lives in context: Perspectives on the ecology of human development* (pp. 423–466). Washington, DC: American Psychological Association.

Steinberg, L., Elmen, J. D., & Mounts, N. S. (1989). Authoritative parenting, psychosocial maturity, and academic success among adolescents. *Child Development, 60*, 1424–1436.

Parent and Family Involvement

Andrews, D. W., Soberman, L. H., & Dishion, T. J. (1995). The Adolescent Transitions program for high-risk teens and their parents: Toward a school-based intervention. *Education and Treatment of Children, 18*(4), 478–498.

Epstein, J. L. (1986). Parents' reactions to teacher practices of parent involvement. *The Elementary School Journal, 79*, 277–294.

Epstein, J. L. (1987). Parent involvement. What research says to administrators. *Education and Urban Society*, 119–136.

Epstein, Joyce L. (1988) How do we improve programs for parent involvement? *Educational Horizons, 66*(2), 58–59.

Hawkins, J. D., & Catalano, R. F. (1990). Intensive family preservation services: Broadening the vision for prevention. In J. K. Whittaker, J. Kinney, E.M. Tracy, & C. Booth (Eds.), *Reaching high-risk families: Intensive family preservation in human services* (pp. 179–192). New York: Aldine de Gruyter.

Hawkins, J. D., Catalano, R. F., Jones, G., & Fine, D. N. (1987). Delinquency prevention through parent training: Results and issues from work in progress. In J. Q. Wilson, & G. C. Loury (Eds.), *From children to citizens: Families, schools, and delinquency prevention* (Vol. 3, pp. 186–204). New York: Springer-Verlag.

Turnbull, A. P., Blue-Banning, M., Turbiville, V., & Park, J.(1999). From Parent Education to Partnership Education: A Call For a Transformed Focus. *Topics in Early Childhood Special Education, 19*(3), 164–171.

Parent Involvement in Homework

Balli, S. J., Demo, D. H., & Weman, J. F. (1998). Family involvement with children's homework: an intervention in the middle grades. *Family Relations: Interdisciplinary Journal of Applied Family Studies, 47*(2), 149–157.

Community Involvement

Bell, A., & Sigsworth, A. (1987). Education and community development: What can the school do? In A. Bell & A. Sigsworth, (Eds.), *The small rural primary school* (pp. ??–??). Bristol, PA: Falmer Press.

Burch, P., & Palanki, A. (1994). Action research on family-school-community partnerships. *Journal of Emotional and Behavioral Problems, 1*(4), 16–19.

Davies, D. (1991). Schools reaching out: Family, school and community partnerships for student success. *Phi Delta Kappan, 72*, 376–382.

Hill, H., Piper, D., & Moberg, D. P. (1994). "Us planning prevention for them:" The social construction of community prevention for youth . *International Quarterly of Community Health Education, 15*(1), 65–89.

Mattessich, P. W., & Monsey, B. R. (1993). *Collaboration: What makes it work*. St. Paul, MN: Amherst H. Wilder Foundation.

Wehlage, G. G., & White, J. A. (1995). *Citizens, clients, and consumers: Building social capital*. Madison, WI: Center on Organization and Restructuring of Schools.

Notes

Notes

Notes

Notes

Notes

Notes

Notes

Notes

Notes

9781596670136